FULLNESS OF LIFE

FULLNESS OF LIFE

Historical Foundations
for a New Asceticism

by
MARGARET R. MILES

THE WESTMINSTER PRESS
PHILADELPHIA

Book Design by Alice Derr

First edition

Published by The Westminster Press®
Philadelphia, Pennsylvania

PRINTED IN THE UNITED STATES OF AMERICA
9 8 7 6 5 4 3 2 1

Library of Congress Cataloging in Publication Data

Miles, Margaret Ruth.
  Fullness of life.

  Includes bibliographical references and index.
  1. Body, Human (Christian theology)
2. Asceticism. I. Title.
BT741.2.M54   233'.5   81-11535
ISBN 0-664-24389-4   AACR2

CONTENTS

PREFACE

TEXTS OF EARLY CHRISTIAN authors are unanimous and emphatic in identifying what they received from the historical appearance of Jesus Christ simply as "life." Repeatedly and insistently the earliest descriptions of Christian experience say that doctrine, liturgy, and even Christian community were all ways of expressing what they experienced as a tremendous surcharge of life. Early Christians described their sharp, quick sense of life in strong language:

> True life comes from partaking in God.
> *Irenaeus*

> God takes away the deadness in us.
> *Origen*

> Only they can think of God without absurdity
> who think of him as life itself.
>
> *Augustine*

The fourth-century Eucharistic prayer of Serapion of Thmuis expresses the center of the Christian experience: "We beg you, make us truly alive."

This book will explore descriptions of historic Christian authors from Ignatius of Antioch to Thomas Aquinas of the relationship of body and soul and their suggestions that the Christian life centers around the task of "keeping body and soul together." Since the world is not in pressing need of more books, the only excuse for writing another book is the conviction that its content is important to the life of its readers. The process of researching, pondering, and formulating this book has involved, for me, nothing less than a correction of my "double ignorance," inherited from a popular tradition which assumes the negativity of historic Christian authors' attitudes to the human body. My surprise in finding that Christian authors were not only intensely interested in but also overwhelmingly affirming of the body as an integral and permanent aspect of human being has led both to this effort to communicate what I discovered in historic texts and to my confidence that providing access to ideas of the body in historical Christianity is worth another book.

I am grateful to the students at Harvard Divinity School with whom I investigated the texts and explored the ideas which appear in this book. I appreciate the generosity of Professor John J. Connelly of St. John's Seminary in reading and commenting on the chapter that treats St. Thomas Aquinas, and to Professor Stanley S. Harakas, Dean of Holy Cross Greek Orthodox Seminary, for his consideration of the material of the Eastern section of the early medieval chapter. And I am constantly and continuingly grateful to my friend and husband, Professor Owen C. Thomas of the Episcopal Divinity School for his attention as I talked out these ideas over many dinnertimes and for his valuable knowledge and insight. This book is part of my continuing longing to understand, intellectually and experientially, the injunction of I Cor. 6:20: "Glorify God, and bear God in your body."

MARGARET R. MILES

INTRODUCTION

We beg you, make us truly alive. *Serapion of Thmuis*

I

FAR FROM IGNORING the meaning and value of the body, Christian authors have written voluminously about embodiment from the earliest times. But although these writings are both many and explicit, historical theologians have seldom analyzed what part ideas about the body played in the theological agendas of their authors. Scholars have taken too literally the counsel of some historic figures to "pay no attention" to the body, failing at the same time to notice that the author himself actually paid a great deal of attention to it. Neglect of the subject of the human body in Christian theology, then, is an important aspect of the context of this book.

Moreover, slenderness of scholarly interest in the history of the idea of the human body has given rise to the stereotypical belief that all Christian thinkers have urged repression of bodily pleasures, energies, and needs, and disaffirmed the body itself. The sources of this general impression are too varied and often obscure to consider directly. Rather than do so, I will attempt to correct here a widespread contemporary misunderstanding, in this regard, of those authors most central to the Christian tradition. We will need to discuss further the components of this misunderstanding but for now it is enough to mention it as a second aspect of the context of this book.

Finally, there is a concern with "keeping body and soul together" implicit in contemporary thought which is evidenced in the insistence of the liberation theologies that altering inhuman political structures and unbearable living conditions is fully as important as giving people new and better ideas. This concern characterizes feminist theology's awareness of the pervasive way sexist language and social structures condition human beings and alienate them from their own bodies and from others as embodied. It is also manifest in the demand of sexual-preference minorities that theology recognize and respect their experience, in the struggle in the field of medical ethics to develop medical care for *whole* human beings, and in the concern of ecologists to make us aware of the connection between abuse of our own bodies and that of the earth. These concerns frequently rest on the assumption that we have received an overwhelmingly negative view of the human body from Christian history, and the question then asked is how these views have been perpetrated on us.

In this regard contemporary authors often rely upon secondary treatments of classic figures like Augustine, Calvin, or Aquinas which display a few clearly damning quotations from the historic texts, and are then ready to "document" blame and get on with the constructive tasks of contemporary theology. Hasty judgments of historic authors by writers interested only in contemporary problems are the third element of the context in which this is written.

These three problematic elements of the cultural and intellectual context of this book, then, are scholarly neglect, popular misunderstanding, and the distorting treatment of historic authors by those whose main concern is contemporary questions.

II

The first methodological assumption which those who invest in intellectual pursuits tend to make is that intellectuals single-handedly originate ideas. Thus, for example, when we find a certain idea especially constricting, our first instinct is to blame the historic thinker who formulated it. This ignores the extent to which ideas arise in response to their context and are, in this sense, "occasional." An idea will strike people as important or useful only if it has an affinity with its context of thought. This is as true of critical ideas as it is of those related to popular consciousness. We have only to consider the variety and range of ideas of the body in our own time to recognize that those in conflict with our current cultural assumptions, asceticism for example, are quickly dismissed. An author, of whatever vintage, receives ideas from both history and culture and depends upon culture to determine their usefulness. Thus responsibility for an idea does not rest totally with the person who gave it its standard formulation; it also has to do with the way this formulation responded to a cultural situation.

A second major methodological difficulty in interpreting historic texts is the assumption that authors of other times operated with the same central issues and agendas that we do. For example, when we find in the devotional literature of a particular period repeated injunctions to cultivate an attitude of repentance for one's sins, we understand these instructions as if given to ourselves and consider them oppressive. Freud has so thoroughly indoctrinated us about the destructive aspects of our dealings with our children, lovers, communities, and natural environment that our problem is not to recognize these aspects, but to seek forgiveness for them and the courage to continue. For us it is hard to imagine people for whom the recognition and acknowledgment of sins were a necessary part of self-understanding and who were unaware of and/or insouciant about their own destructiveness. Such a different psychic structure is difficult for us to conceive of, but respect for the historic texts requires us to understand their agendas as in most cases sophisticated attempts to diagnose and prescribe for the specific spiritual difficulties of the people of that period.

Thirdly, a historic text very seldom manages to reconstruct for us that liveliness and excitement of historic people who wanted, as we do, to feel "truly alive," and who understood the connection of this sense of aliveness to holding ideas that led in fruitful directions. An adequate method for dealing with historic texts requires that we assume the author aimed to change the cultural context in the direction of greater life. It may seem difficult for us to interpret the "martyrdom consciousness" of early Christian authors as directing their culture toward lifefulness, but in Chapter II we will examine strong reasons for doing so.

Fourthly, one of the pitfalls in any survey of thought is that only those single aspects of a thinker's work will be explicated which are most distinctive or which later events require that we describe as part of a "development toward." We can excuse the distortions caused here by our narrowness of focus by remembering that it also illuminates certain aspects of a thinker's work whose neglect is far more distorting. Our focus on ideas of the body will indicate the degree of a thinker's interest—or the *lack* thereof—in the meaning and value of the human body.

Finally, we need to acknowledge the difficulty of understanding an element of Christian thought that has been so widely misunderstood. Misunderstanding is far more difficult to rectify than confessed lack of understanding because we think we *do* understand. Plato called this *double* ignorance. This book is a contextual analysis of the views of those Christian thinkers who have been most widely and deeply influential on Christian evaluations of the meaning of the body. The dismantling of misunderstanding it will leave to the reader. At this point, I simply post warning that we must be prepared to be startled with what we find when we look carefully at historic Christian views of the body. We must be prepared to recognize and confess what one historian has called the "profound unhistoricity" of our ideas about history. The anonymous collection of ideas about the past which we have received in a nonsystematic way from our intellectual environment very frequently supports such misunderstandings of traditional Christian thinkers. We are often amazed on closer examination to find that a very different, if not opposite, picture emerges from that of the popular "tradition" we have received and appropriated.

III

As mentioned earlier, part of the intellectual context to which this book responds is the method of those contemporary authors who go to the primary sources seeking only proof texts for their own views about the body. To determine the meaning of the texts with any accuracy requires that several questions be asked which will bring us closer to the intentions of the authors of those texts.

The first of these concerns the "occasion" of the text. This question considers the social and cultural condition of the author's time, the immediate impetus for writing, the amount and quality of his education, and the style of discourse he uses. Answering this question could demand years of study and the learning of several languages, or simply a few minutes' reflection on what one already knows of the time and what major psychological differences might complicate *our* understanding of the text. The next important question is about the author's anthropology, how parts or functions of the human being are described, defined, and valued. We need also to consider whether this anthropology is explicit or whether we need to piece it together from the text. Finally, we must ask what the author's central theological agenda is. This may be a direct response to a situation, a challenge, or a debate, or it may be the result of the author's concern that an important feature of Christian belief or practice is being largely ignored or repressed. Where, for example, Christian authors admonished their readers to "pay no attention to" the body, we will need to interpret this counsel in the light of their repeated insistence that in their culture concern about the body has consumed most or all of the soul's attention and energy. As moderns who enjoy a predictable supply of food, clothing, and shelter which we purchase rather than grow, make, or build, we may find it difficult to understand the extent to which the necessity to satisfy bodily needs could easily become the central, and only, concern of historic human beings.

IV

When we turn from methodological questions to the content of historical theologies of the body, we notice very different—and sometimes apparently conflicting—statements not just in different authors but in works by the same author. For example, we may read in Tertullian: "To such a degree is the flesh the pivot of salvation, that since by it the soul becomes linked with God, it is the flesh which makes possible the soul's election by God."[1] But we also find in Tertullian exhortations to asceticism and martyrdom that appear to devalue bodily existence. Is he confused and inconsistent? This apparent inconsistency is not peculiar to Tertullian, but occurs in most historic authors, who could insist on the goodness and even the beauty of the body while yet aware, as were pagans of the time,[2] that bodily practices affect the state of the soul, and that ascetic practices could be used to focus and intensify its energy. The "opposableness" of body and soul was too thoroughly experiential to be questioned. Thus, when Christian authors were writing practically, they emphasized the importance of the body as a useful "tool" of the soul. Often modern interpreters are confused by this apparent contradiction between philosophical affirmation of the body as the good creation of a good God, and an emphasis on ascetic practices which appear to assume the fundamental enmity of body and soul.

Yet we must be prepared, I think, to accept that for several historic authors philosophic affirmation and experiential dualism were not in contradiction. Typically, Christian authors insist that what is good for the soul *is* what is good for the body, so that, far from implying a pejorative view of the body, its "best interests" are served in practices that enhance the soul's energy. Augustine wrote:

> If we seek what is best for the body, determined reason forces us to say: it is whatever makes the body to be at its best. But of all things that enliven the body, none are better or more primary than the soul. Thus, the

> highest good of the body is not its desires, nor its speed, nor absence of
> pain, nor its strength, nor its beauty, nor whatever else is counted among
> the goods of the body, but, indeed, the soul. For the very presence of the
> soul offers the body all the things that were mentioned as well as that
> which excels them all, namely, life.[3]

The problem for traditional Christian thinkers is how to connect the
body, with its inflexible life cycle and intimate affiliation with mortality,
to *life*—animation, momentum, and orientation—which by definition is
a property of the soul.

This brings us to a second problem regarding the content of
statements of historic authors about the meaning and value of the body.
We must take time to look carefully at what a particular author defines as
"body." If we read, for example, that the body is a "stinking corpse," we
immediately take that to be a pejorative statement. Yet the author may
simply be offering a definition of what *he* is calling "body." Augustine,
typical in this respect of Christian authors up to the time of Descartes,[4]
defines the "body" as without animation, psychological predicates, or
feeling, i.e., as if anesthetized, without the soul. Deprived of the soul's
presence the body is literally a "corpse." The body is what is dissected in
an autopsy or buried at death. We are heir to Descartes's definition of
body as an entity that breathes, sleepwalks, possesses involuntary
response mechanisms like stretching out the hand to ward off a blow,
and even walking or singing. If this is our definition of body, we will find
an explicit devaluation of the body in the statement of ancient authors
that the body is a "stinking corpse." Yet Descartes's "body" is not the
definition Augustine had in mind when he described the body as a
"corpse." Thus, it is productive to assume, in the light of the constant
metaphysical affirmation of the body by Christian authors, that when we
read a statement that strikes us as obviously pejorative regarding the
body, its very obviousness must be a warning to be prepared to explore
further why the statement was made. Often, the author will complicate
the task by using different definitions of "body." Sometimes within the
same work "body" will be used as synonymous with "corpse" or with the
technical theological term "flesh," while elsewhere "body" will appear
carelessly used in the sense of the animated, ensouled body. We are safe
in assuming that when a statement about the "body" is pejorative,
"corpse" is what is designated, while if the statement is affirming, the
ensouled "body" is intended.

Finally, a complicating feature of our study is the presence of a sliding scale of valuations of the body that can be documented in all the figures we will discuss. Although no Christian author can completely ignore or misinterpret Christian doctrines that insist on the goodness and permanence of the body as an essential part of human being, a range of valuations is possible. The author may employ the rhetorical device of using the body as *foil* to demonstrate the greater beauty and value of the soul. Or he may present the body as *problem*, or the *condition*, of human learning, trial, salvation, and resurrection to eternal life.

Thus far we have spoken of aspects of the philosophical description of the body by Christian authors. When we approach their practical descriptions of forms of ascetic practice we will see what a bewilderingly wide range of these practices there is. I will not be arguing that *all* of the asceticism in Christian history is equally "Christian," valid, and useful, but rather I will describe four historic models of the goals and methods of ascetic practice that do seem to me to be valuable, and ignored. Estrangement from Western Christian history, at least partially due to its caricaturization as opposed to the body, has meant that we have not been able to use practices and insights for the care of our souls that traditional authors found useful. Many people are beginning to be aware, for example, that there are forms of bodily discipline that are clearly beneficial and energy-producing for both body and soul. Often these people have explored bodily disciplines in the context of non-Western religions because Western forms of ascetic practice have been seen as "masochistic," and Eastern forms have been idealized as "in touch with" the body. We must take a closer look at asceticism as one of the most adamantly maintained aspects of Christian tradition.

We are becoming aware in our time both of the importance of questions relating to embodiment and of the way in which biblical and historical treatments of questions relating to the body influence the cultural and intellectual milieu in which we live and the means we take to illuminate our situation. And so the final section of this book will offer practical proposals for integrating the uses of traditional Western Christian tools for the care and treatment of our souls and bodies. We can learn from historic Christian authors by using their insights to correct our cultural and psychological blind spots. But we may also find we need to reject some of their methods because of cultural assumptions and models that are no longer productive, even though we can appreciate their usefulness to the people who formulated them.

The final purpose of this book, then, is to reclaim as accurately as possible historic Christian ideas of the meaning and value of the body, and to show how these are related to the goals of traditional asceticism. And we will ask ourselves, once we have gathered these, what their underlying assumptions and models were, in order to determine for ourselves what aspects of traditional Western asceticism we can use. For example, at one and the same time we may find some of the assumptions indefensible and problematic, the models tending to the fragmentation of the human being, but the goals attractive and valuable. We then need to rescue what we can use and are in need of from those assumptions and models we cannot accept.

The old asceticism will not serve us; its assumptions are often exaggeratedly dualistic,[5] and its too-frequent model is rape of the body's vitality for the benefit of the soul. Yet we are as much in need of methods to concentrate our energies as were those who created Western asceticism. We need, then, to construct with the tools recommended to us by the past a "new asceticism," some form of attentiveness to life styles and practices which will care for both soul and body and which are equally beneficial to each. Our closing chapter will sketch such a "new asceticism."

We have begun by describing the advantages in constructing a "new asceticism," but there is another pressing reason to pursue this task. The inevitable result of misunderstanding an aspect of our past that has shaped us culturally is that we begin unconsciously to assimilate the very aspect we consciously deny. Our aversion to historic asceticism has blinded us to many unrecognized forms of asceticism in our own culture. Modern life displays an underground asceticism that relies upon the model of rape of the body's vitality to a degree that even the most extravagant Western asceticism did not, viz., to the point of causing death. Why can we not recognize the old ascetical model of subordinating the body to the soul in such prevalent practices in our culture as alcoholism, promiscuity, overeating, drug dependence, overwork, an inhuman pace of life, and environmental pollution? Yet all these, in their different ways, are the results of the soul's attempt to assert its life, however briefly and however destructive to the body this may be. These unacknowledged asceticisms take the self-deceiving form of indulgence, the new face of the old asceticism in our time. But they do not make us feel alive. Addictive, they require the continual staving off of habituation by steadily increasing dosages of power, sex, and possession. The unconscious asceticism of our time that dulls and damages both souls and bodies can begin to be overcome if we can recover an understanding of historical Christian asceticism. Only through the perspective of accurate historical research can we gain the self-knowledge consciously to affirm—or to alter—the formative role that asceticism has had on the very structure of our souls and bodies.

I

MARTYRDOM, GNOSTICISM, AND THE EARLY CHURCH

THE HUMAN BODY was a central theme of early Christian thought. By the fourth century the doctrines of creation, incarnation, and resurrection of the body forced Christians to recognize that the classical anthropology of a stratified human being with irrational soul stacked on top of body, and a further rational soul stacked on top of that, did not fit comfortably with the strong affirmation of the body implicit in the earliest Christian doctrines. But even before philosophical assumptions received from classicism were examined directly, in the second and third centuries several pressing problems caused Christian writers to undertake a strenuous rehabilitation of their views of the body. First, the Gnostics' disparagement of the body as the creation of an evil power and constant source of evil and difficulty for the soul brought men as dissimilar in their concerns as Tertullian and Irenaeus, Clement of Alexandria and Ignatius of Antioch, to describe a specifically Christian understanding of the meaning and value of the body. Arguing Christian doctrines against the Gnostics, they affirm the goodness of the body unambiguously, sometimes quite extravagantly. Thus, Tertullian writes:

> Is it conceivable that God has consigned to some very cheap receptacle the reflection of his own soul, the breath of his own spirit, the workmanship of his own mouth, and has thus, by giving it an unworthy lodging, definitely brought about its damnation? But did he give it a lodging, or not rather entwine and commingle it with the flesh? Yes, in such close concretion that it may be considered uncertain whether the flesh is the vehicle of the soul or the soul the vehicle of the flesh. Yet, though it is more creditable that the soul, as more akin to God, is the rider and the master, this also redounds to the glory of the flesh, that it both contains the soul which is God's kin, and puts it in possession of that selfsame mastery. . . . Moreover, if it is through the flesh that all things

are subject to the soul, they are subject to the flesh as well: you must of necessity have for partner in your use of a thing the instrument by which you use it. Thus the flesh, while it is reckoned the servant and handmaid of the soul, is found to be its consort and coheir: if in things temporal, why not also in things eternal?[1]

And yet almost every Christian writer of the period before the Peace of the Church in A.D. 313, confronted by the practical reality of spasmodic but persistent persecutions which increased in severity right up to the time of Constantine, also wrote an admonition to martyrdom. Was the human body valued as a metaphysical entity but in practice thought of as worthless? It is difficult to know how to interpret such statements as the following statement of Tertullian:

> Come now, what think you of the flesh when for the faith . . . it is dragged into public and fights it out exposed to popular hatred, when it is tormented in prisons by loathsome exile from light, by lack of ornament, by squalor, filth, abusive food, free not even in sleep, since even on its bed it is chained, and is mangled even by its mattress—when next even in daylight it is rent by every contrivance of torture, when at length it is destroyed by execution. . . . Yea, most blessed is it, and most glorious.[2]

Also, we need to understand the martyrdom consciousness of the early church and to see its relationship to metaphysical affirmation of the body if we are to understand asceticism. The emphasis on asceticism that began with Clement of Alexandria and became a constant theme of Christian theology after the third century was a direct continuation of the martyrdom consciousness of the times of persecution. The seventh-century text *Barlaam and Joasaph* makes the connection explicit: Asceticism "arose from men's desire to become martyrs in will that they might not miss the glory of them who were made perfect by blood."[3] The "daily martyrdom" of the ascetic life became the image of Christian perfection in times when persecution had ceased. Origen even laments the temporary passing of the time of persecution because of the sincerity of Christian profession which the threat of martyrdom fostered:

> Those were the days when Christians really were faithful, when the noble martyrdoms were taking place, when, after conducting the martyrs' bodies to the cemeteries, we returned thence to meet together, and the entire church was present without being afraid, and the catchumens were being catechized during the very time of the martyrdoms and while people were dying who had confessed the very truth unto death.

. . Then we knew and saw wonderful and miraculous signs. Then there were true believers, few in number, but faithful, treading the straight and narrow way which leads to life. But now, when we have become many, out of the multitude which profess piety there are extremely few who are attaining to the election of God and to blessedness.[4]

These two external pressures and dangers—Gnosticism and the threat of martyrdom—forced Christians of the early church to think and write about the human body. From these struggles to formulate a convincing and consistent Christian view of the body, the thinkers of the fourth century received both their problems and their tools for working under the differing pressures of their own time. In this chapter we will explore first the intellectual pressure from Gnosticism and the response of two patristic authors to it. Secondly, we will discuss the idea of martyrdom and the "martyrdom consciousness," and an attempt will be made to show the relation of the response to Gnosticism to the Christian affirmation of the abrupt and painful sacrifice of the body in martyrdom. Finally, the teachings of Clement and Origen on the subject of the body will be discussed as they both summarize earlier views and formulate some important and influential emphases for the fourth century and the medieval period.

I

The Gnostic movement—an anachronistic name for a number of religious systems that taught the cosmic redemption of the human spirit through insight into its condition of entrapment in the physical world and through metaphysical knowledge of its true home in the spiritual world—was the most intimate and therefore the most threatening theological opponent of the early church. Both the Christian movement and the various Gnostic movements grew up in a culture that agreed on a normative human experience of painful disjunction between the spiritual and the physical dimensions of human life. That it was the duty of a religious system to address this disjunction, offering not only a satisfactory explanation for it but also a treatment, was tacitly accepted by both Christianity and Gnosticism. The Gnostic systems addressed the experience of disjunction by focusing on it, providing a cosmology that supported and explained it. They made the painful experience of disjunction itself the impetus for the rejection of the physical world of objects and bodies, which they understood to be the essential movement of the salvation of the soul. The special attraction of the Gnostic systems was their satisfactory explanation of the existence of evil, and its location in an "enemy" that is neither vague nor distant, but a constant and necessary condition of human life—embodiment in the material world. The constant opposition to an enemy which lies so close—one's own body—generated an energy whose existence goes a long way toward explaining the popularity of the Gnostic systems.

The fall of the soul into the alien environment of world and body can be redeemed, according to the Gnostics, by acknowledging this alienation from the material world: "for matter is not capable of being saved." Incarnation is always a catastrophe. Yet we must be careful not to caricature the Gnostic consciousness; there is, in some of the Gnostic texts, a strong sense of embodiment as the condition that provides—precisely because of its pressing painfulness—the necessary stimulus for redirecting attention and energy to the soul; physical life is ambiguous in that it can lull a person to sleep in the transitory world of the senses. But it can also jerk a person abruptly into consciousness of his condition. In this sense, physical life is a usable—because painful—condition.

Christians struggled to describe the same cultural and psychological experience. The *Epistle to Diognetus* formulates the experience of a disjunction between soul and body which its author finds to be a perfect metaphor for the Christian's experience of disjunction between God and the world:

> What the soul is in the body, that Christians are in the world. The soul is dispersed through all the members of the body, and Christians are scattered through all the cities of the world. The soul dwells in the body but does not belong to the body, and Christians dwell in the world but do not belong to the world. The soul, which is invisible, is kept under guard in the visible body; in the same way, Christians are recognized when they are in the world, but their religion remains unseen. The flesh hates the soul and treats it as an enemy, even though it has suffered no wrong, because it is prevented from enjoying its pleasures; so too the world hates Christians even though it suffers no wrong at their hands. . . . The soul is shut up in the body, and yet itself holds the body together; while Christians are restrained in the world as in a prison, and yet themselves hold the world together.[5]

The sense of "holding together" uncomfortably disparate aspects of human being could not be described by Christians in the Gnostic version of an antagonism of soul and body based on different and antagonistic origins of soul and body. The doctrines of creation, of incarnation, and of resurrection of the body required Christians to reject the Gnostic explanation of the experience of pain and evil. And these Christian doctrines, which insist on the integration of the human body as an essential and permanent aspect of human being, were exactly the doctrines that Christian writers constantly developed and emphasized in response to what was, in the cultural consciousness of the early Christian centuries, the highly attractive Gnostic description and solution.

We will look at the responses of two Christian authors as representative of the problems and attempts to offer solutions of second- and third-century Christians. From different perspectives, Tertullian and Irenaeus formulated strengthened doctrines of human embodiment as reinterpreted in the light of the incarnation of Jesus Christ. A scanning of Tertullian's treatises *Adversus Marcionem, De carne Christi,* and *De resurrectione carnis* and of Irenaeus' *Adversus haereses,* Book V, will give a sense of just how concerned about the body and Christian interpretations of the body these authors were. We will explore Tertullian's insistence, largely against Marcion, on the goodness and permanence of human incarnation as it is validated by the incarnation of the Word, and Irenaeus' concern to demonstrate the essential significance of Christ's fully human incarnation in refuting the docetism of various Gnostic groups.

Tertullian's polemic against Marcion focuses some of Tertullian's strongest insistence on the value of incarnation. Although Marcion was not, in some respects, a typical Gnostic—he did not, for example, take interest in cosmological speculation, but rather in ethics and Scriptural exegesis—he shared a dualistic view of anthropology and a dualistic Christology with Gnostic thinkers. Tertullian developed his accounts of the incarnation and resurrection in polemic against Marcion, who had been dead since A.D. 160, and whom Irenaeus had already vigorously combatted. Marcion apparently had an especially hostile view of the body and the physical world, which he supported by citing the existence of reptiles and insects, and the "uncleanness" of sex and childbirth. In order to vindicate the purity of Christ, Marcion had denied that Christ's birth was a characteristically human birth. Tertullian, too, saw the question of the human birth of Christ as pivotal to the question of his incarnation, but argued the appropriateness of human birth to one who shared the condition of human beings in suffering and death as well as in birth:

He chose rather to be born, than in any part to pretend—and that indeed
to his own detriment—that he was bearing about a flesh hardened without
bones, solid without muscles, bloody without blood, clothed without the
tunic of skin, hungry without appetite, eating without teeth, speaking
without a tongue, so that his word was a phantom to the ears through an
imaginary voice.[6]

The characteristic origin of a human life in the world was necessary if
Christ were to die a human death because "between nativity and
mortality there is a mutual contract."[7]

Tertullian's fully incarnational view of Christ was aided by his premise
that soul, like body, is corporeal and requires a *place* to exist. Using the
Stoic idea that the criterion of existence is bodily existence and the
criterion of bodily existence is ability to affect other bodies, the soul,
which very evidently affects and moves its body, must necessarily "have
a something through which it exists"—its body. Lacking a corporeality
that meets the conditions of existence, Christ could have effected no
salvation for the human race—an obviously and notoriously embodied
species! An "angelic" Christ could only have redeemed disembodied
souls, and indeed this is the intent of Marcion's claim that Christ was not
truly born, did not truly suffer nor truly die:

And since they assume it as a main tenet, that Christ came forth not to
deliver the flesh, but only our soul, how absurd it is, in the first place, that
he made it into just that sort of bodily substance which he had no intention
of saving.[8]

Tertullian considered the efficacy of Christ's redemption of the human
race to be dependent on his assuming the fully human condition as
guaranteed by his human birth; Christ's birth, then, is the "certain
proof" of the humanity of his flesh.[9] Tertullian's description of the details
of the birth process and nourishment by lactation has the flavor of a
taunt, addressed to Marcion, but directed to contemporary followers of
Marcion, Apelles, Basilides, and Valentinus:

This sacred course of nature, you, O Marcion, spit upon; and yet, in what
way were you born? You detest a human being at his birth; then after what
fashion do you love anybody? . . . Well then, loving man, Christ loved
his nativity also, and his flesh as well.[10]

It is important to notice that Tertullian's exaggeration of the
"uncleanness" of birth[11] does not appear in the context of disparaging
human birth; quite the opposite: Tertullian exaggerates "the filthy

concretion of fluid and blood [which is the basis of] the growth of the flesh for nine months long out of that very mire"[12] precisely to serve as an emphasis on the acceptability of human flesh to Christ, who not only considered it worth saving, but took it upon himself. It is ironic, then, that Tertullian is usually quoted as evidence of the existence of strongly pejorative views of the body in early Christian thought. Lifted from their context, his descriptions of birth certainly do seem to support this, but if we read them as Tertullian intended them, they support, rather, his affirmation of the irreducible integrity of all aspects of the body in a human being.

The permanent integration of the body in the most significant possibility of human being—salvation—is Tertullian's theme in his *De resurrectione carnis*. Against Gnostic claims that the body, because of its material substance, cannot be redeemed, Tertullian sets out to demonstrate the body's crucial role in salvation:

> To such a degree is the flesh the pivot of salvation, that since by it the soul becomes linked with God, it is the flesh which makes possible the soul's election by God. *(Adeo caro salutis est cardo, de qua cum anima deo alligatur ipsa est quae efficit ut anima eligi possit a deo.)* For example, the flesh is washed that the soul may be made spotless: the flesh is anointed that the soul may be consecrated: the flesh is signed that the soul too may be protected: the flesh is overshadowed by the imposition of the hand that the soul may be illuminated by the Spirit: the flesh feeds on the body and blood of Christ so that the soul also may be replete with God.[13]

A significant development occurs between the time, shortly after his conversion, that Tertullian wrote the *Apologeticus,* and the decade or so later that the *De resurrectione carnis* and the *De carne Christi* were written. The main reason given for the necessity of the bodily resurrection in the early work was the requirement that the whole person receive the judgment of God on her or his bodily acts:

> For that reason men's bodies also will be restored again, because soul without that solid matter, the flesh, is not capable of sensation, and because whatsoever the souls have to suffer by the judgment of God, they have deserved it in association with the flesh: for they were enclosed within the flesh when they did all that they have done.[14]

The changed description of the later works, in addition to being the result of an increased knowledge of Scripture and tradition, was the result of the strong incentive to describe and develop a Christian affirmation of the body against the pressures of the Gnostic groups.

Tertullian's imagery of the appropriateness of the bodily resurrection also changed from the early writing to the later treatises: in *Apologeticus*, Tertullian offered the experiential proof of the rhythm of life and death in the days and seasons of the year; the world itself is, he says, "a signed portrait of the resurrection of mankind":

> Daily the light is slain and shines anew: darkness by the same sequence departs and returns: constellations which have died come to life again: seasons end and begin: fruits ripen and return: certainly grain rises in greater fertility only after it has decayed away and dispersed: all things are preserved by being destroyed.[15]

Although this analogy from the physical world is used again by Tertullian in *De resurrectione* 12, in this treatise it forms a prelude to his vision of the life of the resurrection body, a vision informed by Scripture: "You retain the Scriptures by which the flesh is brought under a cloud: retain these also by which it is made glorious."[16] In his discussion of "Not in bread shall a man live, but in the Word of God," Tertullian reveals his only objection to the present life of the body: the mechanical and automatic character of "the usages of the flesh," the necessity, supported by painful and continuous labor, of nourishment and reproduction. The life of the resurrected body will be altered in only one respect—the body will be freed from the necessities imposed by hunger, thirst, and procreation. It is death which imposes necessity on the body: "For when death has been taken away, neither the supports of livelihood for the preservation of life, nor the replenishment of the race, will be a burden to the members . . . not marrying, because also not dying, [and] submitting to no similar necessity of the corporeal constitution." Discussing the text, "They will be like angels,"[17] Tertullian is emphatic that "he did not say, 'like angels,' so as to deny their humanity, but 'like angels,' so as to conserve their humanity: he did not deprive them of their substance when he added to it a similarity."

The body became, for Tertullian, a person's very self, an intimate and permanent feature of human being. Tertullian again raises the requirement that the body participate in judgment as it has been a full partner in human activity, and it is from this perspective of a strengthened view of the flesh as integral to human being that he describes the members of the body as full partners in this activity: "I for my part am aware that it was not with some other flesh that I committed adulteries, and that it is not now with some other flesh that I am striving toward continence."[18]

> For God's judgment seat demands a person in full being: in full being, however, he cannot be without the members, for of their substances, though not their functions, he consists.[19]

It is important to notice that it is precisely Tertullian's defense—and "glorification"—of the metaphysical status of the human body that requires its participation in judgment and suffering, or in reward as "the Bride of Christ."

> So then the flesh will rise again, all of it indeed, itself, entire. (Resurget igitur caro, et quidem omnis, et quidem ipsa, et quidem integra.) Whatever it is, it is on deposit with God through the faithful trustee of God and humans, Jesus Christ, who will pay back both God to man and man to God, spirit to flesh, and flesh to spirit. . . . But it is the flesh which is the bride, for in Christ Jesus it has taken the Spirit for bridegroom.[20]

The corollary of Tertullian's strengthened description of the total and permanent integration of the body is insistence—in fully "fleshed out" detail—on the participation of the body in judgment, suffering, and reward. This is a startling, and, to us, not altogether comfortable, consequence of an integrated description of human being. The Gnostics, who held that the body could be neither saved nor damned, but was at death simply discarded, never took pleasure in fantasies of the torments of the damned as Tertullian did.[21] Rather, the Gnostics' sacrifice of the body enables them to hold the pleasant view that the resurrection has already taken place in the resurrection of the soul to transformed life in Christ.[22] "The heretics," Tertullian writes, rely on the "simplicity and agreeableness of their pronouncements and the familiarity of their thoughts, and are considered the more trustworthy in that they define things open and apparent and generally known: whereas divine reason is in the marrow, not on the surface, and is frequently in opposition to things as they seem."[23]

The psychological experience of a painful disjunction between the body *as we know it* and the soul was a normative and pressing experience for Tertullian as it was for the Gnostics. His "rehabilitation" of the body was a strenuous effort to overcome a predilection for the Gnostic diagnosis and prescription. He certainly found warrant for this rehabilitation of the body in Scripture, but the fact that his ascetical and ecclesiastical convictions led him to leave the Catholic Church for the Montanist sect, and finally to leave that sect in order to found the Tertullianist sect, indicates the extreme concern he felt to reject—as much as possible in this life—the "necessities" of the body and to approximate the life of the resurrection in which the characteristic "activity" of the body will be rest. This is, in fact, precisely the way in which Tertullian describes ascetic practice: allowing the body a temporary rest[24] which is a "release from"[25] constant activity. By accustoming the body "not to feel the need of"[26] food and sex, for example, through fasting and celibacy, Tertullian anticipates the resurrection state of the body. This is certainly a positive view of asceticism which is consonant with Tertullian's metaphysical affirmation of the body.

Irenaeus' work *Adversus haereses* addresses the Gnostic claim that the incarnation of Christ was "in appearance only" and that "Jesus" and "Christ" were entities without inner coherence. Irenaeus' theology centers on the "recapitulation" by the incarnated Word of the normative event in which the human race, in Adam, was confronted with a choice of either obedience and life or disobedience and death. Christ, by reenacting this paradigmatic situation, reversed the choice and thereby made available to the human race the life it had lost in the original situation. Life can only go on from the point at which it was arrested, and the work of Christ effectually freed the life that had been paralyzed by the choice of disobedience. But in order to accomplish this freeing act, Christ must have recapitulated in himself the whole human being.

> But if [the human race] was taken from the dust, and God was its Maker, it was incumbent that the latter also, making a recapitulation in himself, should be formed as man by God, to have an analogy with the former as respects his origin. Why, then, did not God again take dust, but wrought so that the formation should be made of Mary? It was that there might not be another formation called into being, nor any other which should require to be saved, but that the very same formation should be summed up in Christ, the analogy being preserved.[27]

The flesh of Christ and its corollary, the bodily existence of human beings, are thus crucial to Irenaeus' theology. In his insistence that the human person is not constituted only by soul and spirit but also—and irreducibly—by body,[28] Irenaeus underlines the full embodiment of Christ as crucial to his salvific act:

> For if he did not receive the substance of flesh from a human being, he neither was made man nor the Son of man; and if he was not made what we are, he did no great thing in what he suffered and endured. But everyone will allow that we are a body taken from the earth, and a soul receiving spirit from God. This, therefore, the Word of God was made, recapitulating in himself his own handiwork.[29]

So intimate is the connection between the salvation of the whole human person and the human body of Christ that only the incarnation demonstrates the creation of human beings in the image of God. As the twentieth-century philosopher Ludwig Wittgenstein would later say, "What can be shown cannot be said."[30] Before the incarnation, "it was *said* that human being was created after the image of God, but it was not yet *shown*," but when "the Word of God became flesh," he confirmed both the image and likeness of God. If, Irenaeus says, "the flesh were not capable of being saved, the Word of God would in no wise have become flesh."[31] But Irenaeus will go further: "Now the final result of the work of the Spirit is the salvation of the flesh."[32]

Just as the activity of Christ would not be complete if it were not a fully embodied act of salvation, so the salvation of the whole person would be incomplete if only the soul and spirit were saved.[33] The body, made in the image of God, is necessarily included; the alternative to claiming and integrating one's body, Irenaeus writes, is not—as the Valentinians claim—becoming a "spiritual person," but becoming merely "the spirit of a person": "The saved person is a complete person."[34]

A different ethic and a different view of the resurrection is required if the body is to be integrated into the salvation of the whole person. Irenaeus presents the Christian life as an immediate transition from viewing the body as the vehicle of sex to seeing the body as one's very self. The Gnostics, Irenaeus asserts, because of their failure to integrate the body in a description of salvation, have no foundation for a consistent and adequate ethical practice:

> There are those among them who assert that man who comes from above ought to follow a good course of conduct; wherefore they do also pretend a gravity with a certain superciliousness. The majority, however, having become scoffers also, as if already perfect, and living without regard, yea in contempt of that which is good, . . . allege that they have already become acquainted with that place of refreshing which is within their Pleroma.[35]

Irenaeus, wishing to show the greater consistency and value of the Christian integration of the body, describes the "lusts of the flesh" in a way that carefully avoids any necessary connection between the "works of the flesh" and the body. The "lusts of the flesh" are the destructive *activities* in which a person indulges and not "the substance of the body":

> Now we have washed away, not the substance of our body, nor the image of our primary formation, but *the former vain conversation*. In these

members, therefore, in which we were going to destruction by working the works of corruption, *in these very members are we made alive* by working the works of the Spirit.[36]

The culmination of Irenaeus' task, "the exposure and refutation of knowledge falsely so called," is an extended argument for the necessity of the body's participation in the resurrection of the dead. Refuting one of the Gnostics' favorite proof texts, "Flesh and blood cannot possess the kingdom of God," Irenaeus patiently explains that it is not only possible that the body will share in the final salvation of the whole human being in resurrection, but that the body is, in fact, the "lost sheep which the Lord came seeking." Since the body is the only part of the human being that can accurately be said to die, it is the only part that is resurrected from the dead.[37]

> But this event happens neither to the soul, for it is the breath of life; nor to the spirit, for the spirit is simple and not composite, so that it cannot be decomposed, and is itself the life of those who receive it. We must therefore conclude that it is in reference to the flesh that death is mentioned; which flesh, after the soul's departure, becomes breathless and inanimate, and is decomposed gradually into the earth from which it was taken. This, then, is what is mortal. And this it is of which he also says, "He shall also quicken your mortal bodies."[38]

Since "flesh and blood procure for us life,"[39] it is appropriate that the healing miracles of Christ offer an anticipation of the transformation to health of the whole human being in the resurrection:

> For what was his object in healing portions of the flesh, and restoring them to their original condition, if those parts which had been healed by him were not in a position to obtain salvation? . . . Or how could they maintain that the flesh is incapable of receiving the life which flows from him, when it received healing from him? For life is brought about through healing, and incorruption through life. He, therefore, who confers healing, the same does also confer life; and he who gives life also surrounds his own handiwork with incorruption.[40]

Irenaeus' teaching on the Eucharist reflects and supports his emphasis on the concrete salvation of the whole human person. The nourishment of the body and blood of Christ initiate and guarantee the vivification of the body which will be complete and permanent in the resurrection:

> How can they say that flesh passes to corruption and does not share in life, seeing that flesh is nourished by the body and blood of the Lord? . . . As

the bread, which comes from the earth, receives the invocation of God, and then it is no longer common bread, but Eucharist, but consists of two things, an earthly and a heavenly; so our bodies, after partaking of the Eucharist, are no longer corruptible, having the hope of the eternal resurrection.[41]

Irenaeus' rehabilitation of the idea of the body as an integral part of the human being leads[42] to a different location for evil than that of the Gnostics. If the body is not the cause and locus of evil, how can evil be understood? Irenaeus identifies the devil and the kingdom of Antichrist as the source of the pain and evil of the earthly condition of human beings. The power of evil is temporary, within God's jurisdiction, and will finally be overcome. Mortal life, then, is not to be seen as a condition of inevitable participation in the evil material world as it was for the Gnostics; Irenaeus describes the life of the Christian as "a commencement of incorruption," a condition in which Christians are "accustomed gradually to partake of the divine nature." The physical creation, then, the natural world and the body are not impediments to "partaking in the divine nature," but are permanent features of the resurrected existence:

For it is just that in that very creation in which they toiled or were afflicted, being proved in every way by suffering, they should receive the reward of their suffering; and that in the creation in which they were slain because of their love to God, in that they should be revived again; and that in the creation in which they endured servitude, in that they should reign. For God is rich in all things and all things are his.[43]

Finally, Irenaeus criticized the remedy that the Gnostic authors offered for the pain of mortal life. Irenaeus characterized the followers of Valentinus as teaching that:

The knowledge of the ineffable greatness is itself perfect redemption. . . . Knowledge is the redemption of the inner person. This, however, is not corporeal, since the body is corruptible; nor is it animal, since the soul is the result of a defect, and is, as it were, the habitation of the spirit. The redemption must therefore be spiritual; for they claim that the inner spiritual person is redeemed through knowledge, that they possess the knowledge of the entire cosmos, and that this is true redemption.[44]

Irenaeus found this claim for the regenerative effect of knowledge to be inadequate and presumptuous. For Christians, the body is no longer the convenient scapegoat for the destruction, waste, and frustration of mortal life, but becomes the medium and the method of entrance into eternal life. In addition, salvation itself comes to the Christian in a manner congruent with the touching fragility of the body. In a passage in which Irenaeus discusses the concrete effect of the Eucharist, in which "the substance of our flesh is increased and supported," Irenaeus quotes II Cor. 12:9, "The strength of God is made perfect in weakness," concluding:

> Having received the body and blood of Christ . . . our bodies, being nourished by it, and deposited in the earth, and suffering decomposition there, shall rise at their appointed time, the Word of God granting them resurrection to the glory of God.[45]

The salvation of the whole person is effected in this way, Irenaeus says, because the *process* of death and resurrection is the only possible mode of fully human learning; the strength of God, "made perfect in weakness," is the *bodily* appropriation of knowledge which the Gnostics rejected and scorned: "And might it not be the case, perhaps, . . . that for this purpose God permitted our resolution into the common dust of mortality, that we, *being instructed by every mode,* may be accurate in all things for the future, being ignorant neither of God nor of ourselves?"[46] It is precisely this aspect, the humble willingness to undergo learning in which the bodily process is the paradigm and condition of learning, which Irenaeus finds lacking in the Gnostics' claim to knowledge. Their knowledge is useless and abstract, omitting, as it does, the human body from salvation and resurrection.

II

The second major impetus for careful consideration of the meaning and value of the human body by the Christian church of the first three centuries was the threat of martyrdom.[47] Ironically, a group of people whose central experience was a surcharge of life were forced by the threat and reality of martyrdom to define the role of the body in participation in Christian life. Texts of early Christian authors say repeatedly that Christian ideas, doctrine, liturgy and literature and iconography are all ways of trying to formulate and express the experience of early Christians of an orientation to the source of life. Before Christianity was knowledge, before it was rectified moral commitments, even before it was community, Christian faith was explicitly an orientation to the source of life. Their language is strong and explicit: Ignatius of Antioch and the *Didache* both present an experience simplified to the essential choice between the "way of life" and the "way of deadness."[48] "True life," Irenaeus wrote, "comes from partaking in God."[49] The Eucharistic prayer of Serapion of Thmuis, "We beg you, make us truly alive," formulates the early Christians' experience of what Christian faith could do for them.

This strong sense of lifefulness led early Christians to locate the enemy of human life, not in death, but in deadness: "He does away with the . . . deadness in us,"[50] Origen wrote.

> All who wish to follow him can do so, though overcome by death, since death has now no strength against them: for no one who is with Jesus can be seized by death.[51]

It may be that there is an element of "denial of death" in these and similar statements by early Christians. We are accustomed to associating denial of death with an identification of the body with suffering and evil and the release of the soul from this body at death. This is not the foundation of the early Christians' "denial of death"; their willingness—even eagerness—to undergo martyrdom was not support-ed by a view of the body as worthless or negative. From the earliest accounts of martyrdom, a constant theme is the preciousness of the martyrs' bodies both before and after their death. *Beforehand,* "the faithful always vied with one another as to which of them would be the first to touch his body."[52] *After* the martyr's death, the community tried to take away the corpse in order "to have fellowship with his holy flesh," although often, as in Polycarp's case, they were prevented from doing so by the destruction of the corpse by Roman authorities: "So we later took up his bones, more precious than costly stones and more valuable than gold, and laid them away in a holy place."[53] It is clear that martyrdom was not rationalized as ridding oneself of a worthless or evil aspect of human being.

We find, rather, three repeated rationales for the value that early Christians placed on dying as a martyr for the Christian faith in the early apologies and *Actae*. The first rationale for the martyr's sacrifice is that martyrdom is the "perfect" participation in the suffering and death of Christ. This has two dimensions: on the one hand, the martyr suffers with—or shares—the suffering and death of Christ; on the other hand, it is not the martyr who suffers the pain and ignominy of a gruesome public death, but Christ who suffers in the martyr's stead. Here the account of the protomartyr, Felicitas, during a difficult childbirth in prison, is significant:

One of the warders said to her: "You who so suffer now, what will you do when you are flung to the beasts?" And she answered: "Now I suffer what I suffer: but then Another will be in me who will suffer for me, because I too am to suffer for him."[54]

In the martyrdom of Polycarp, the elements of participation in the passion of Christ are especially clearly drawn. Both the external events and the responses of Polycarp are self-consciously shown to be proof of a "martyrdom conformable to the gospel." Polycarp "waited to be betrayed, just as the Lord did"; details, such as the name of the chief of police—Herod—who arrested Polycarp, his betrayal by members of his own household, and the instigation of the Jews, are noted. Polycarp's response to his own arrest was not a pious formula, but a self-conscious repetition of Christ's words in the garden of Gethsemane, "God's will be done." The miracles surrounding his death—such as the fire that formed a wall around him and would not consume his body—emphasize further Polycarp's participation in the suffering of Christ, even to the stab wound from which he died, just as Christ's side was pierced with a sword.

The second rationale for the value of martyrdom which the early *Actae* suggest is that of "release from a wicked and lawless life."[55] Clearly these Christians who valued being "truly alive" found in the structures of the surrounding culture the "deadness" reflected and caused by the hideous distortion of human values.[56] One of the motivations for martyrdom was escape from such a world. They eagerly sought release to a world in which human values, especially and insistently the beauty and goodness of the body, are eternally affirmed: the body is returned "risen and glorious." The death of the martyr, then, becomes the occasion for the dramatic conversion of values that have been inverted in Roman culture.

The inversion of ordinary language in the letters of Ignatius of Antioch dramatizes the inversion of values in late Roman society: "Do not hinder me from living," Ignatius pleads—in chains, and on his way to martyrdom in Rome—to the Roman Christians who want to intercede for the commutation of his death sentence. "Do not wish for my death; now I am beginning to be a disciple; only let me attain to Jesus Christ."[57] Ignatius twisted the ordinary meaning of "life" and "death" into their opposite meanings in order to try to express the intensity of his longing to be released from a world in which "nothing you see has any value."[58]

One would have to tell gruesome and tasteless stories of late Roman

Sunday afternoon family entertainment at the Colosseum in order to evoke a feeling of horror and disgust which in some way adumbrates the horror and disgust of the early Christians for a culture that anyone with human values could only want to be away from. It is this feeling that provides the context for the martyrs' willingness—even eagerness—to be free of their culture. We should notice and acknowledge the element of rage in the *Actae* and apologies of the early church. This anger is evident in the taunts with which Christians greet the crowds in the arena, in the scorn with which they regard their pagan contemporaries, and in the belligerent acts and words that often prompted their arrest. An example may help us to understand this aspect of the martyrdom consciousness of early Christians. Camus, in *The Stranger*, describes the feelings of his hero about his imminent execution: he hopes, Camus writes, that when he steps up to the guillotine he will be greeted with mocking shouts of execration. This will make it easier to die. The early Christian martyrs certainly had conditions that made death-into-life maximally attractive, and their zest in flinging taunts to the crowds who jeered while they suffered indicates their consciousness of the usefulness of both their rage and the cruel rage of the crowd in helping them accept and embrace death.

This aspect of the martyrdoms has been largely neglected owing to our preference for seeing the entire motivation of the Christian's acceptance of martyrdom in terms of their love for Christ and for each other. We must, I think, manage to hold together both this aspect of real anger and rejection of a culture that rejected them and the love that made martyrdom acceptable. The motivation of love is the only viable explanation for the martyrs' apparent joy so often described by eyewitnesses; their apparent insensibility to pain was clearly the result of *amor nec stupor*, love rather than insensibility. Yet recognizing their eagerness to gain eternal life should not prevent our acknowledging their angry rejection of life on earth.

Finally, there is the repeated suggestion that the sufferings of the martyrs occur "no longer in the flesh."[59] Even in prison, awaiting execution, in some accounts the martyrs experienced a consciousness that was absolutely discontinuous with ordinary consciousness. There is agreement in the *Actae* that a person cannot approach shameful martyrdom with every evidence of peace and joy except as God grants this consciousness; it is emphatically not something a person can "do." If such a state of consciousness is not granted, the confessor will not be able to maintain her or his confession by sheer "willpower." The generosity of the protomartyrs to confessors who lapsed is evidence that they did not regard martyrdom as "heroic" in the normal sense. Those "unready, untrained, and still feeble, unable to bear the strain of a great contest,"[60] gave the protomartyrs "sorrow and grief unmeasurable," but they bore them no resentment; they were simply not yet "there," and apparently this carried no personal guilt or blame. Rather, the protomartyrs saw those who denied their faith as helpless victims of the devil, who had lulled them into "unconsciousness." Biblias, for example, in the *Letters from the Churches of Lyon and Vienne,* denied the faith, but was then tortured for information about other Christians. In the midst of this torture she suddenly "returned to her sober mind and woke, as it were, from a deep slumber . . . and from this moment she confessed herself a Christian and was added to the company of martyrs."[61]

These ways of describing the meaning and value of martyrdom, while in a sense denying death, in that physical death is no longer the enemy of human life, do not imply any negative ideas or feelings about the human body. It was, in fact, precisely the abuse of the body in late Roman culture that the Christians protested. Rationales for the acceptance of martyrdom revolve around the Christian affirmation that death is not to be understood as "the release of the soul from the prison house of the body," as it was for pagans; rather, death's meaning is summed up in Polycarp's prayer just before his martyrdom:

> I bless thee, because thou hast deemed me worthy of this day and hour, to take my part in the number of the martyrs, in the cup of thy Christ, for resurrection to eternal life of soul and body in the immortality of the Holy Spirit, among whom may I be received into thy presence this day as a rich and acceptable sacrifice.

The "denial of death" of these texts is an aspect of the martyrs' intoxication with the life of Christ with which they felt themselves so intimately connected. The constant theme of the *Actae* is that succinctly expressed by one of the letters from the churches of Lyon and Vienne: "They [the martyrs] asked for life and he gave it them, which they shared with their neighbors, and departed for God in all ways victorious."[62]

II

THE ORIGINS
OF CHRISTIAN ASCETICISM

I

THE FIRST CHRISTIAN writer who "placed the ascetic ideal on the same level as that of the martyr,"[1] Clement of Alexandria, presents a far more subtly nuanced view of the human body than those we have explored thus far. His interest in the body was the result of concerns other than those which motivated some Christian authors to refute Gnosticism or rationalize martyrdom. The apocalyptic expectations of the earliest Christians, the sense of living in the "last days," and the orientation to martyrdom—the personal form of apocalypse—were being somewhat modified in parts of the Roman Empire. In Alexandria, a catechetical school in the shadow of the great university of Alexandria trained the most promising young men of the time in a course of instruction which began with the study of geometry, physiology, and astronomy, advanced to the study of philosophy, and culminated in the study of theology. Such a graded study implies, if not leisure, at least a pace which demonstrates an expectation that they would not be suddenly interrupted by martyrdom.

Clement of Alexandria, second head of the catechetical school, was interested in a quality of human life which was permeated with "the true life" because of its inclusive orientation to "him who is the Life indeed, owing to whom we live the true life."[2] Clement described the quality of this life thus:

All our life is a festival: being persuaded that God is everywhere present on all sides, we praise him as we till the ground, we sing hymns as we sail the sea, we feel his inspiration in all that we do. [We] enjoy a greater intimacy with God, being at once serious and cheerful in everything, serious owing to our thoughts being turned towards heaven, and cheerful as we reckon up the blessings with which God has enriched our human life.[3]

The first descriptions of asceticism occur in the context of this interest in Christian life on earth. We will examine two representatives of the school of Alexandria in order to understand, in the context of their theological concerns, the role of the human body in their philosophical work and in their ascetical instructions. Both Clement and Origen began with a cultural and philosophical heritage of ambivalence about the meaning and value of the body. One of the major unsuccessful projects of the middle Platonists had been the resolution of Plato's conflicting suggestions concerning the origin and cause of human embodiment.[4] An experiential dualism, formulated in its strongest philosophical statement by the most influential mind of the second century, Numenius, and in its strongest religious and metaphysical statement by various Gnostic groups, was the mood of the third-century intellectual world.

In addition, pagans and Christians alike shared the intellectual assumption that any description of human good must be integrated into a description of the cosmic order. The language of description of human being was spatial, reflecting a concern to place it in a cosmic setting. Clement's essay "On Spiritual Perfection"[5] describes a Christianized cosmic order in which a universe created by the power of the Word depends on "one original principle." It is a graded, ordered series, reaching from the "one original principle" through "the first and second and third generations," the angels; "and so, even down to ourselves, ranks below ranks are appointed, all saving and being saved by the initiation and through the instrumentality of One." Clement uses Plato's image of the magnet[6] drawing iron particles through iron rings to describe the "attraction of the Holy Spirit" by which those who have chosen virtue and contemplation are irresistibly drawn to "the highest mansion."[7]

The good for human being, in this metaphysical scheme, consists of beginning where one is, that is in the lower ranks of creation, to discipline the mind by knowledge and the body by virtue and thereby to begin to move back up the ranks to "that which is lovely." A characteristic Platonic ambivalence about the body and the material world is preserved in Clement's description: while each level of the cosmos has its own validity and value, the assumption that the human person is cosmically defined by the level which attracts his or her attention and affection places responsibility on that person to resist attachment to the lower orders and to explore and strengthen a connection with the higher levels.

This task and responsibility implies the need for struggle and a

method. Such a struggle is laborious, but "within our power."[8] Before
the incarnation of the Word, the methods provided were the
commandments to the Jews and philosophy to the Greeks, both of
which, Clement grants, can lead to "perfection." But the presence of the
Word on earth in Jesus Christ provided a dramatic "short-cut to
perfection"—salvation through faith.[9] We will need to discuss in more
detail the task of the individual in beginning the ascent to the "highest
mansion," the vision of God, but for now we will note only that the
individual must—and can—choose to improve his or her life—and
cosmic position—by increasing in knowledge and virtue:

> The soul that at any time improved as regards the knowledge of virtue and
> increase in righteousness, should obtain an improved position in the
> universe . . . a preeminence at once of knowledge and of inheritance.
> These saving revolutions are each severally portioned off, according to the
> order of change, by variety of time and place and honor and knowledge
> and inheritance and service, up to the transcendent orbit which is next to
> the Lord, occupied in eternal contemplation. . . . Whatever is possessed
> of virtue changes to better habitations.[10]

This cosmic setting is the context of Clement's view of the body and
asceticism. Metaphysically described, the human body attaches a
person to the material world and so provides both the condition and the
problem of human being. The problem of the body is its distance from
the "one original principle." Yet Clement is painstakingly careful to give
no blame to the body; his treatise "On Marriage" begins with a rejection
of the Platonic and Marcionite view that the body is the "tomb of the
soul."[11] After enumerating passages from Plato, Marcion, and others in
which this evaluation is given, Clement objects that an unambiguously
pejorative view of the body does not yield a principle on which virtuous
activity can be based; all the heresies, he says, teach either

> that one ought to live on the principle that it is a matter of indifference
> whether one does right or wrong, or they set *too ascetic a tone* and
> proclaim the necessity of continence on the ground of opinions which are
> godless and arise from hatred of what God has created.[12]

"Hatred of what God has created" does not provide a stimulus for the
choice of using the soul's energy for the ascent to the vision. Quite the
opposite. The "evidence of his capacity to receive knowledge," and
therefore the starting point[13] of the true Christian gnostic, is precisely
"admiration for creation":

> Starting with that admiration for the creation which he brings with him as evidence for his capacity to receive knowledge, he becomes an eager disciple of the Lord. . . . *His admiration prompts him to believe.* Proceeding from this point he does his best to learn in every way.[14]

The ability to admire is exactly the opposite of the condition of attachment which Clement describes as slavery and "bondage to pleasure."[15] If one's attachment to physical pleasures is encouraged and strengthened by unmodified indulgence in pleasures, one becomes a slave, and loses one's capacity for admiration, enjoyment, and gratitude for the created world. Admiration requires freedom:

> He . . . has given us this free and sovereign power and has allowed us to live as we choose, not allowing us to become enslaved and subjected to necessity by our acts of choice and rejection.

And the condition of freedom is detachment:

> We ought to behave as strangers and pilgrims, . . . as people who are not *passionately attached* to the created world, but use it with all gratitude and with a sense of exaltation beyond it.[16]

What is it that keeps the soul "attached" to the created world through its investment in physical pleasures rather than engaged in exploring and strengthening its connection to the "one original principle"? Clement answers, in his metaphor of the magnet—the Holy Spirit—and its drawing power:

> As then the remotest particle of iron is drawn by the influence of the magnet extending through a long series of iron rings, so also through the attraction of the Holy Spirit the virtuous are adopted to the highest mansion, and the others, in their order, even to the last mansion: but they that are wicked from weakness . . . neither keep hold themselves nor are held by another, but collapse and fall to the ground, being entangled in their passions.[17]

The passions, although "not a bodily thing," belong to the body; the passions occur, Clement says, "because of the body"[18] and "tie" the whole person "to the ground."[19] Attachment to physical pleasures is the slavish subjection which Clement identifies as the cause of deadness, the opposite of the Christian experience of life. When we ask what possibility human freedom has to participate fully in the "true life" of "him who is the Life indeed," Clement paints for us a picture of the gnostic Christian.[20] A (to us) most startling connection is drawn between the passionless condition of the "true gnostic" and the "change from death to life" that is the center of the Christian's experience. *Apatheia*, apathy, is the condition of the Christian life because it does not participate in the deadness caused by attachment to physical pleasures and the created world:

> For both the Gospel and the apostle command us to bring ourselves into captivity and put ourselves to death, slaying the old man which is being corrupted according to its lusts and raising up the new man from the death of our old perversion, laying aside our passions and becoming free from sin. This is that which was signified also by the law when it commanded that the sinner should be put to death, viz., *the change from death to life*, that is the apathy *[apatheia]* which comes from faith.[21]

Once this *deadness* is eliminated, even death can be nothing but a "discipline" for the Christian. The enemy of Christian life is no longer death but deadness:

> Whether disease or accident befall the gnostic, aye, or even death, the most terrible of all things, he continues unchanged in soul, knowing that all such things are a necessary result of creation, but that, even so, they are made by the power of God a medicine of salvation.[22]

A further problem of the body is the inadequacy of the model of bodily growth and "perfection" when this model is used to inform the soul's activity in ascending to the vision of God. For Clement, the contemplative vision is the normative human activity, the activity in which human self-actualization occurs. This "apprehensive vision of the pure in heart" is the lifework of the gnostic Christian.[23] It is a vision which is possible in this life, we should notice, and therefore embodiment does not present an absolute limit, but the paradigm of the body's natural growth "to perfection" does not provide a natural instinctive model for the activity of contemplation by which the gnostic attains "the perfection of one who in love is full grown":[24] "For neither are we born virtuous, nor is virtue a natural aftergrowth as are parts of the body."[25] Rather, the body as implicit model misleads the would-be comtemplative. There is nothing automatic or natural about the quest of the "lover of truth." The lover of truth needs "energy of soul" to reach the goal[26] and "cleansing and training in order to overcome the inertia caused by weakness and ignorance, the 'two causes of failure.' "[27] Corresponding to ignorance and the weakness that results from attachment to the objects of the physical world, then, there are two disciplines. For ignorance, the knowledge provided by Scripture is the remedy; for weakness, there is the training or discipline of ascetic practices. The two disciplines, that of the soul and that of the body, are inextricably linked.

Christ has come, Clement says, not to bring us the abstract knowledge of the Gnostic sects, but the knowledge which

> easily transplants a person to the divine and holy state . . . and by a light of its own carries him through the mystical stages till it restores him to the crowning abode of rest, having taught the pure in heart to look upon God face to face with understanding and absolute certainty.[28]

It is the knowledge which provides energy to change that is necessary to the true gnostic:

> Knowledge comes from the fruit and from behavior, not from talk and from blossom. We say that knowledge is not mere talk, but a certain divine knowledge . . . which reveals all that is in a state of becoming, enables man to know himself, and teaches him to become possessed by God. . . . Let them not call bondage to pleasure freedom, as if bitterness were sweet. We have learnt to recognize as freedom that which the Lord alone confers on us when he liberates us from lusts and desires and the other passions.[29]

Once the attachment to physical pleasures is loosened, the magnet—the Holy Spirit—can freely draw the gnostic to the "lovely itself, [but] to attain to the knowledge of God is impossible for those who are still under the control of their passions."[30] We saw earlier that Clement described the incarnation as a "short-cut" through the laborious ascent to God implied in Plato's metaphor of the many links of the magnet. Because of the increment of energy in the incarnation of the Word, in which the drawing power of the High Priest who stands at the pinnacle of the cosmic order[31] was brought to the level of human beings, the gnostic is "drawn" with incredible speed and confidence:

> Those gnostic souls are so carried away by the magnificence of the vision that they cannot confine themselves within the lines of the constitution by which each holy degree is assigned . . . but being counted as holy among the holy, and translated absolutely and entirely to another sphere, they keep on always moving to higher and yet higher regions, until they no longer greet the divine vision in or by means of mirrors, but as loving hearts feast forever on the uncloying, never-ending sight, radiant in its transparent clearness, while throughout the endless ages they taste a never-wearying delight.[32]

The absolute condition for this cosmic "translation," which Clement calls "being assimilated to God," is that the gnostic Christian has been "subdued by training to a passionless state." But the state of "apathy" is insistently not a state of feeling nothing. The exterior form of this passionless state is "gentleness, kindness, and a noble devoutness";[33] the feeling tone of this state is that of being "truly alive," of the "change from deadness to life."

What part does the body play in this process? Does the body carry only the negative role of providing passions which the soul can struggle against?

> Without the body how could the divine plan for us achieve its end? Surely the Lord himself . . . came in the flesh. . . . [And] does not the Savior who heals the soul also heal the body of its passions? But if the flesh were hostile to the soul, he would not have raised an obstacle to the soul by strengthening with good health the hostile flesh.[34]

Here we are at the heart of Clement's ambivalence about the body. The body is the condition of the gnostic Christian's "shortcut," and yet attention and energy are required if the passions that occur "because of the body" are not to capture the soul's energy and "bind it with the fetters of the flesh."[35] The body has the potential of being either "temple or tomb"; it can be invested either in the passions that attach the person to physical pleasures or it can become the connection of the whole person to the source of life:

> In addition to this he [the apostle] makes the point still clearer by saying emphatically, "The body is dead because of sins," indicating that if it is not the temple, it is the tomb of the soul. . . . For when it is dedicated to God, he adds, the spirit of him who raised Jesus from the dead dwells in you, who shall make alive your mortal bodies through his Spirit dwelling in you.[36]

Temple or tomb—Clement's ambivalence about the human body is distilled in this phrase. Only the discipline of the soul—knowledge—and the discipline of the body—training—can effectively move the whole person toward the vision of God. Both, we have said, are interwoven: discipline must be "based on knowledge," and the result of this conscious discipline of the body is that "habit is changed into nature." It is only in this dialectic of spiritual advance that knowledge comes to be not merely intellectual grasp, but integral to the whole person—"nature": "In such a one his knowledge becomes an inseparable possession, like weight in a stone."[37]

Clement's ideal is integration, not rejection of the physical aspect of human being in favor of the intellectual. When the body is ordered to the connection of the whole person to life, the discipline of the body provides the soul with energy. Clement's image of the participation of the body in the soul's quest retains his sense of the ambiguity of the body which is a problem for—and the condition of—the contemplative vision:

> For this reason also we raise the head and lift the hands in the closing outburst of prayer, following the eager flight of the spirit into the intelligible world: and while thus *we endeavor to detach the body from the earth* by lifting it upwards along with uttered words, *we spurn the fetters of the flesh* and constrain the soul, winged with desire of better things, to ascend into the holy place.[38]

Notice that when the body is detached from its attachment to physical pleasures and connected to the soul's activity of contemplation, not the body but the "fetters of the flesh" are spurned; the soul does not attempt to detach itself from the body, but integrates the body in its "eager flight." Embodied life participates in "Life indeed."

Clement's picture of the Christian life as irreducibly involving and including the body forms the context for his discussion of every other aspect of it. No activity is too trivial to elicit Clement's opinion on how it should be managed, from behavior at banquets to sneezing! Humorous as this instruction in the *Paedagogus* may be, its underlying rationale is perfectly consonant with Clement's idea that nothing about the Christian life is unimportant. "Asceticism," then, in Clement, does not have the meaning which usually we ascribe to it, i.e., practices, different from the course of ordinary daily life, which require effort and concentration. For Clement, asceticism is from the outset an intimate feature of the Christian life. It involves, on the one hand, the freedom of the person: "For this is the law from the beginning, that he who would have virtue must choose it."[39] On the other hand, Clement says that the life of spiritual discipline requires that one regard the conditions and events of life as God-given:

> For continence is not merely a matter of sexual abstinence, but applies also to other things. . . . There is also a continence of the tongue, of money, of use, and of desire. *It does not only teach us to exercise self-control; it is rather that self-control is granted to us*, since it is a divine power and grace.[40]

There is no contradiction in Clement's affirmation of both the God-givenness of the conditions and events of one's life *and* the active engagement in using these conditions as spiritual discipline, that is, as forms in which to exercise the choice of exploring and strengthening the connection of the whole person to life. Asceticism is the choice to stop temporarily the outflow of the soul's attention and affection to the objects of the physical world, and to turn this attention and affection to one's connection with "divine power and grace."

In this endeavor, the human body bears a significance not seen in earlier writers: "In us it is not only the spirit which ought to be sanctified, but also our behavior, manner of life, and our body."[41] The aim of asceticism is integrating the body into the program of the soul, and not "treating one's body roughly."[42]

If we look carefully at the passages in which Clement discusses continence and marriage, we see that his criterion for both conditions is the same. Both states are God-given and "within our power"[43] and are to be regarded as spiritual discipline. It is not the external condition that is significant, but the acceptance of the condition as God-given and the activity of working with the condition in which one finds oneself. Clement's celebrated "generous" view of marriage comes from this principle. Whatever condition provides the most varied and strenuous "training" for a particular individual is the best condition. According to this principle, marriage can be more useful than continence:

> True manhood is shown, not in the choice of a celibate life; . . . [but] by him who has trained himself by the discharge of the duties of husband and father and by the supervision of a household, . . . by him who in the midst of his solicitude for his family shows himself inseparable from the love of God and rises superior to every temptation which assails him through children and wife and servants and possessions. . . . He who has no family is in most respects untried.[44]

Renunciation as such, in Clement's view of asceticism, is emphatically not the point.[45] Quoting Paul's "Let no one disqualify you by demanding self-imposed ascetic practices . . . and severe treatment of the body,"[46] Clement says that it is more difficult and more valuable to accept the condition of full participation in the management of sex, power, and possessions, and to learn from this training to engage one's whole life in the love of God. Neither is "willpower" the characteristic activity of the God-lover. Clement specifically differentiates Christian asceticism from the "human ideal" that "one should fight desire." "For a soul that has to concentrate upon endurance is lost."[47] For the person to whom God has given the condition of continence, our ideal is not to experience desire at all. Our aim is not that while a person desires he should get the better of it, but that he should be continent even respecting desire itself. This chastity cannot be attained in any other way except by God's grace.[48]

By this insistence that asceticism, the Christian's "detachment from the earth," is not to be achieved by gritting one's teeth, Clement aims to correct the idea of a joyless struggle to separate one's self from the physical pleasures which—if "concentrating upon endurance" is one's mental state—nevertheless occupy one's attention and interest. The material world, even riches,[49] and the bodily beauty of one's friends,[50] can be enjoyed with gratitude when all of human life is ordered to "Life indeed." The specific psychological quality of life as spiritual discipline is joy; the most ordinary and humble activities of everyday life are marked by this quality:

> Throughout the day and night he is filled with joy uttering and doing the precepts of the Lord, not only at dawn on rising, and at midday, but also when walking and lying down, dressing and undressing, . . . carrying God within him and being carried by God.[51]

II

In Clement's concern to describe the Christian life in a way which recognized the significance of bodily activities and conditions, we have seen the transition from the martyrdom orientation of the early church to the "daily martyrdom" of the ascetic life, that is, the life in which every circumstance and condition becomes a spiritual discipline. In Origen, the most influential Christian author on ascetic monasticism, Clement's view is strengthened, both in its ambivalence about the body and in its emphasis on human embodied existence as a perfectly accurate reflection of the condition of the soul. Embodiment is the strenuous learning experience that instigates the soul's quest for the highest good of the whole human being.

For Origen, as for Clement and the authors of the early period, the enemy of human life is not death but deadness. Christian faith is quite simply a change from deadness to life:

> If by participation [in the Word] we are raised from deadness and enlightened, . . . it is clear that through him we are made rational through divine inspiration; . . . he does away with the irrationality and deadness in us.[52]

Death no longer threatens the Christian whose participation in the life of Christ has already placed her or him in life:

> Such people accept the putting away of the body . . . without distress or emotion when the time comes for them to put off the mortal body by what is commonly regarded as death.[53]

The life in Christ is "stronger than the authority of death, and so much stronger that all who wish to follow him can do so, though overcome by death, since death has now no strength against them: for no one who is with Jesus can be seized by death."[54]

Like Clement, Origen begins with the insistence that a human being is capable of and responsible for using human life to come to the full participation in the vision of God that is eternal life:

> Let us therefore take up eternal life. Let us take up that which depends upon our decision. God does not give it to us. He sets it before us. "Behold, I have set life before thy face." It is in our power to stretch out our hand, to do good works, and to lay hold on life and deposit it in our soul. This life is the Christ who said, "I am the life." This life is that which now is present in shadow but then will be face to face. . . . What sort of life shall we live when we are no longer living under the shadow of life but are in life itself. . . . Let us haste towards this life, groaning and grieving that we are in this tent, that we dwell in the body. So long as we are present in the body we are absent from the Lord. Let us long to be absent from the body and to be present with the Lord.[55]

This quotation brings together Origen's concern for the freedom of the human person, his judgment that the highest value of human life is the vision of God, and his sense of the body as a problem: "So long as we are present in the body we are absent from the Lord." We will examine the interrelationship of these concerns, but we must first take note of several important aspects of the study of Origen's theology.

In A.D. 533, fifteen condemnations were issued by the fathers of the Second Council of Constantinople of views alleged to have begun with Origen. Subsequently, his writings were systematically destroyed, so that few remained in the original. Latin translations done by opponents like Jerome and friends like Rufinus of Aquileia survived and form the main body of texts of Origen we have. A description of the difficulties caused by this condition of the primary texts cannot detain us here. Rather, we must emphasize Origen's concern for orthodoxy and his own description of his theological assumptions. "As for myself," Origen wrote,

my wish is to be truly a man of the Church, to be called by the name of
Christ and not by the name of any heretic, to have this name which is
blessed over all the earth; I desire to be and to be called a Christian in my
works as in my thoughts.[56]

No Christian author was more devoted to the study of Scripture, and his
influence in this area was determinative throughout the medieval
period. Yet Origen had a speculative theology which began from the
assumption that "points not clearly set forth in Scripture" may be,
subject to clear limitations, speculated upon. His thoughts in this regard
are the result of his longing for a connected body of doctrine:

Much more, and beyond all comparison, does the mind burn with
unspeakable longing to learn the design of those things which we perceive
to have been made by God. This longing, this love has, we believe,
undoubtedly been implanted in us by God; and as the eye naturally
demands light and vision and our body by its nature desires food and
drink, so our mind cherishes a natural and appropriate longing to know
God's truth and to learn the causes of things.[57]

Although our interest in Origen's teaching is centered on his reflections
on points "not clearly set forth in Scripture,"[58] we must remember the
enormous body of Scriptural translations and exegeses that formed the
bulk of Origen's lifework. Speculative work occupied only a small
fraction of his energy and time, but it permeates all his Scriptural work.

The limitations of theology for Origen are: (1) that nothing may be
attributed to God which is incompatible with the Scriptural descriptions
of his goodness,[59] and (2) that "we must be careful always to strive to
preserve reverence to God and his Christ and to avoid subordinating
reverence to intellectual inquiry."[60] The specific point at which Origen
sacrificed his love of speculation to "reverence" was his teaching on the
incarnation of Christ. Despite the apparent difficulties (and here the
fragmentary condition of Origen's Latin and Greek texts makes an
accurate assessment of Origen's ideas extremely difficult), with his
doctrines of creation, with resurrection of the body, and with a
description of the Trinity, Origen is insistent on the real embodiment,
real activity, and real suffering of Jesus Christ.[61] This affirmation, as we
will see, led him to modify significantly his idea of the possibilities for
human being.

Origen's speculative tendencies are at their strongest in the areas of his
thought where the human body receives attention. We must understand
Origen's ideas of the body in the context of his deep impulse to understand

human life in its cosmic setting. Although alien to modern theological speculation, this was shared by philosophers and religious people of his time, an excitement with bold visionary constructions of the total scheme of things. Origen wanted to see the shape of human life within a context no smaller than the universe and no more limited than endless time.

Within this, Origen shows an ambivalence about the human body which we will examine by looking at his anthropology and at those Christian doctrines which prompted his effort, namely, the doctrines of creation, resurrection, and the incarnation. We shall then briefly explore the rationale for asceticism which made Origen highly influential to the ascetic movements in the following centuries.

Origen's anthropology, as clearly as it can be determined by a careful reading of his *On First Principles*, considers human beings to be a combination of spirit, soul, and body. Soul is the locus of a choice between identification with the spirit or identification with the flesh. His usage is derived from Scripture:

> When it is said that the flesh lusteth against the spirit and the spirit against the flesh, the middle position is undoubtedly occupied by the soul, which either acquiesces in the longings of the spirit or else inclines to the lusts of the flesh. If it joins itself to the flesh, the body becomes one with it in impurity and lust, but if it associates with the spirit, the spirit will become one with it.[62]

Here we have the Pauline description of a struggle of the spirit, that aspect of the human being which listens and speaks to God—and the "flesh," that aspect which has become disoriented and involves the whole human in a struggle to possess finite objects. It is clear that, for Origen, the blame for this fleshly existence does not belong to the body.

> In its own proper nature [the body is] a dead thing, which is only said to possess a mind or a wisdom which is "at enmity with God" or which "wars against the spirit" in the same way as if one were to say that the actual flesh has a voice which protests against being hungry or thirsty or cold, or against enduring discomfort in any respect whatever.[63]

Origen is concerned that language which implies enmity between spirit and flesh should not suggest to the "simple believer" that a neutral soul is pulled in different directions by forces residing in spirit and flesh. Rather, the soul *turns toward* different objects as an act of free choice: "It must not be supposed that there is one life acting in opposition to another."[64] The soul determines the direction of its attention and affection, subject only to the necessity of caring for the needs of the body. Care for the needs of the body does have the potential of distracting and diverting the soul from single-minded concentration on "things that are divine and profitable for eternity."[65] Yet this view of the body as problem occurs in a context in which Origen is setting forth alternative views of the role of the body, and it is not clear that it is a view with which he is fully comfortable.

This view may be seen in exemplary form in Origen's frequent references to the body as "shadow" of the soul. In his anthropology it is the mind which is accurately said to be in the image of God; the body is at the bottom of the hierarchy of human being:

> The marks of the divine image in man may be clearly discerned, not in the form of his body, which goes to corruption, but in the prudence of his mind, in his righteousness, his self-control, his courage, his wisdom, his discipline.[66]

It is in the mind that humankind possesses a consanguinity, a blood relationship with God; the place of the body is that of "shadow" of the mind. In his treatise *On Prayer*, Origen describes the ambiguity of this term. On the one hand, "all bodily and material things, of whatever kind they may be, have the value of an unsubstantial and feeble shadow." The gifts of God which are of greatest value and for which we should pray are not the shadows, but the real thing. Yet

> with the gift of the object, we received also its shadow. . . . Bodily things are the most natural accompaniments of the great and heavenly "spiritual gifts.". . . We must pray, therefore . . . concerning the pre-eminently and truly great and heavenly blessings; and as concerning the shadows that accompany these pre-eminent blessings we must commit this matter to God, who "knows before" we "ask him what things" we "have need of" for the perishable body.[67]

We can begin to reconstruct Origen's view of the body from his teachings on the doctrines of creation, resurrection, and the incarnation. We have said that in Origen's theological system human experience must be explained cosmologically. His doctrine of creation and the fall of the soul into the physical world provides such a cosmic account. The creation of human beings, Origen says, occurred in two stages; in the first stage God created rational natures "after the image and likeness of God,"

> in whom there is nothing material. He who is in the image is not made out of matter. . . . When God made human beings he did not take the dust of

the earth, as he did the second time, . . . but he made him in the image of God, superior to all corporeal existence.[68]

A fragment from the Greek text of *On First Principles* describes the process by which the rational natures came to embodiment:

> By some inclination towards evil these souls lose their wings and come into bodies, first of human beings, then through their association with the irrational passions, after the allotted span of human life, they are changed into beasts; from which they sink to the level of insensate nature. Thus that which is by nature fine and mobile, namely the soul, first becomes heavy and weighed down, and because of its wickedness comes to dwell in a human body. . . . On earth, by means of virtue souls grow wings and soar aloft, but when in heaven their wings sink down through evil and they sink down and become earthbound and are mingled with the gross nature of matter.[69]

Embodiment, then, consists of the combination of a rational nature with "the gross nature of matter." Matter, although created by God as the receptacle for the souls that fell from their first creation, exhibits two characteristics. First, matter has the capacity to reflect with absolute accuracy the "diverse motions of the rational creatures [which] have given rise to the diversity of the world"; in fact, matter formulates this diversity: "The diversity of the world cannot exist without bodies."[70] Secondly, matter exhibits a painful instability that is shared by the bodies which participate in it.[71] These two qualities of matter are inseparable from bodily nature, leading Origen to call the body a "river"; the material substance of the body, he says, changes from one day to the next.[72] This account of creation, though on the surface it appears to be quite pessimistic regarding embodiment, does present it as the precise equivalent of the "diverse motions of the rational creatures." We will need to look at the significance of this aspect of embodiment a bit later.

Now it is necessary, in Origen's theology, that the end of the cosmos be the same as the beginning. Only the Trinity possesses life without a body, and at the end or consummation, Origen says, "God will be all in all." This raises a question about how Origen envisions the body of the resurrection. Origen's answer is not difficult to formulate, but it is hard to see how he arrives at it. His answer is that human beings cannot exist without bodies,[73] but since material substance can "undergo every kind of transformation,"[74] the transformation of the material component in human being into a spiritual component will constitute the resurrection event. The body, its material element transformed, will then share the incorruptibility of the "perfect soul."[75]

This is exactly the spot at which Origen's speculative tendencies are sacrificed to his affirmation of the incarnation of Jesus Christ. The proof and guarantee of the salvation of the body for Origen was the fully human incarnation of Christ, which brought to the human condition of embodiment the possibility of transformation to eternal life. The soul that has "put on Christ" has received the "clothing of the soul" in life; the soul then clothes its body in incorruption; only the incarnation makes this possible:

> Since the body is mortal and has no share in the true life, the bodily form of which we have spoken, a thing by nature mortal, when Christ who is our life shall appear, itself undergoes change from being a body of death and is endowed with life, because by the spirit it has become life-giving spirit.[76]

Origen employs the formula used by Irenaeus and others to insist on both the incarnation of Christ and the full redemption of human being:

> So then our Savior and Lord, wishing to save human beings in the way he wished to save them, for this reason desired in this way to save the body, just as it was likewise his will also to save the soul; he also wished to save the remaining part of human being, the spirit. The whole man would not have been saved unless he had taken upon him the whole man. They do away with the salvation of the human body when they say that the body of the Savior is spiritual.[77]

Origen's insistence, against Celsus, on the full humanity of Christ, locates the soul of Jesus as the connection between God and flesh and parallels exactly his anthropology in which the human soul mediates between spirit and flesh. This emphasis on a connecting activity in Christ is Origen's only "speculative" treatment of the incarnation:

> This soul, then, acting as a medium between God and the flesh (for it was not possible for the nature of God to mingle with a body apart from some medium), there is born, as we said, the God-man, the medium being that existence to whose nature it was not contrary to assume a body.[78]

The human soul, like the soul of Christ, has the capacity to integrate body and spirit in such a concrete and permanent way that even death does not affect this integration. Even the unique property of material existence—diversity—is preserved in the spiritual body of the resurrection, and accounts for the diversity among spiritual bodies.

Originally created without distinction—with perfect equality—souls, by the exercise of their freedom, "either make progress or deteriorate through their negligence."[79] The soul of Christ was a complete participation in God, and,

> clinging to God from the beginning of the creation and ever after in a union inseparable and indissoluble, as being the soul of the wisdom and word of God and of the truth and the true light, and receiving him wholly, and itself entering into his light and splendor, [it] was made with him in a preeminent degree one spirit, just as the apostle promises to them whose duty it is to imitate Jesus that "he who is joined to the Lord is one spirit."[80]

Human souls, because of their freedom, then, participate in life to the degree of "loving affection" with which they cling to Christ:

> By reason of the faculty of free-will, variety and diversity had taken hold of individual souls, so that one was attached to its author with a warmer and another with a weaker and feebler love.[81]

Even the diversity of human beings, which Origen has attributed to the "material element" on which bodies are based, is sustained in the resurrection:

> Just as the saints will receive back the very bodies in which they have lived in holiness and purity during their stay in this life, but bright and glorious as a result of the resurrection, so, too, the wicked, who in this life have loved the darkness of error and the night of ignorance, will after the resurrection be clothed with murky . . . bodies in order that this very gloom of ignorance, which in the present world has taken possession of the inner parts of the mind, may in the world to come be revealed through the garment of their outward body.[82]

Origen's statement that it is the form or essence of the human body rather than the material elements which will be rendered incorruptible in the resurrection is puzzling. The key, I think, to what Origen means by the "form" of the body is found in his discussion of the resurrection. When we look carefully at his description we notice that there is a good deal more concreteness to this form, "which at the resurrection is again thrown round the soul," than the spiritualizing interpretations of Origen's doctrine suggest. It is the form of the body which guarantees that the human body, although "the existing substance does not remain the same in our body for even two days," will maintain a recognizable continuity of features:

The features remain unaltered, and they determine the bodily characteristics of Peter or of Paul. Among such characteristics, scars remain on
the body from childhood, and certain other peculiarities such as moles.[83]

Origen continues: "In the resurrection, the form of the earlier body will
not be lost, even though a change to a more glorious condition takes
place in it. . . . The features which once existed in the flesh will remain
the same features in the spiritual body."[84] Quoting Paul's "This
corruptible must put on incorruption," Origen comments:

> He speaks of "this corruptible" and "this mortal" with the air of someone
> who is as it were touching and displaying something; to what else can it
> apply except bodily matter? The matter of the body, then, which now is
> corruptible, shall put on incorruption when a perfect soul, instructed in
> the doctrines of incorruption, has begun to use it.[85]

The spiritual body, then, composed of the form of the physical body,
will perfectly reflect the state of the soul. And yet it is difficult for Origen
to describe in what sense the human body participates in the
consummation of all things in God:

> But we must not doubt that the nature of this present body of ours may,
> through the will of God who made it what it is, be developed by its creator
> into the quality of that exceedingly refined and pure and splendid body,
> according as the condition of things shall require and the merits of the
> rational being shall demand, . . . when the world was in need of variety
> and diversity, matter lent itself to the fashioning of the diverse aspects and
> classes of things in wholly obedient service to the maker, as to its Lord and
> Creator, that from it he might produce the diverse forms of things
> heavenly and earthly. But when events have begun to hasten towards the
> ideal of all being one as the Father is one with the Son, we are bound to
> believe as a logical consequence that where all are one there will no longer
> be any diversity.[86]

Origen's affirmation of the "development" or transformation of the
human body into a spiritual body which preserves, on the one hand, the
diversity of degrees of integration to the spirit and soul of Christ, and, on
the other hand, eliminates diversity, is difficult. And yet, "no new
bodies are given to those who rise from the dead, but . . . they are to
receive the same ones that they possessed during life, only transformed
from a worse to a better condition."

> Into this condition, then, we must suppose that the entire substance of
> this body of ours will develop at the time when all things are restored and
> become one and when "God shall be all in all."

Origen insists that nothing of the substance—not only nothing of the form—of the human body is lost:

> Our flesh indeed is considered by the uneducated and by unbelievers to perish so completely after death that nothing whatever of its substance is left. We, however, who believe in its resurrection, know that death only causes a change in it and that its substance certainly persists and is restored to life again at a definite time by the will of its creator and once more undergoes a transformation; so that what was at first flesh . . . and was then dissolved through death and again made "dust and ashes" . . . is raised again from the earth and afterwards, as the merits of the indwelling soul shall demand, advances to the glory of a spiritual body.[87]

In Origen's account of the human saga, this final stage is only reached after aeons of training, during which "improvement and correction" will be realized slowly and separately in each individual. Embodiment and participation in the physical world is only the first stage in a process that continues through "infinite and immeasurable ages." Origen is not reluctant to use Plato's description of terrestrial existence as "punishment" to express the meaning of human life: "God therefore made the present world and bound the soul to the body."[88] But Origen's idea of "punishment" is that the soul creates it in completely natural ways:

> Every sinner kindles for himself the flame of his own fire, and is not plunged into a fire that has been previously kindled by someone else or which existed before him. Of this fire the food and material are our sins.[89]

Beginning with the "fall" into the human body, the soul constructs its own learning experience. But all such learning, although painful and not ended by death, is temporary and remedial:

> This training of ours in the body extends over a very long period, namely, up till the time the bodies themselves with which we are encompassed are found worthy of incorruption and immortality.[90]

"God brings fire upon the world," Origen writes, "not as a cook, but as a God who is the benefactor of them who stand in need of the discipline of fire." This purifying fire is to be understood as "chastisement and healing at the same time." But such apparently literal descriptions of punishment are not to be taken literally, Origen says, except "in order to terrify those who cannot by any other means be saved from the flood of their sins."[91]

The training of the soul which begins in this life continues with greater facility after death. Once freed by death from being "shut up within bars of flesh and blood and rendered duller and feebler by reason of association with material substances, souls learn rapidly."

> And so the rational being, growing at each successive stage, not as it grew when in this life in the flesh or in body and in the soul, but increasing in mind and in intelligence, advances as a mind already perfect to perfect knowledge, no longer hindered by its former carnal senses, but developing in intellectual power, ever approaching the pure and gazing "face to face" . . . on the causes of things.[92]

Each stage of the soul's progress unavoidably involves embodiment. It seems clear that Origen taught some form of metempsychosis in which the many bodily conditions of the soul are themselves the discipline that purifies it. The transitoriness of bodies in continuous flux is transformed in Origen's teaching from negative "punishment" to a positive condition for learning.

An interesting result of Origen's description of the learning experience of the soul is his view of the relationship between soul and body. Bodily experience is transferred directly to the soul: "There is punishment, but not everlasting. For when the body is punished, the soul is purified, and so is restored to its ancient rank."[93] Origen, who was not interested in reevaluating the low position of the body in the hierarchy of body, soul, and spirit, did not feel a need to theorize about physical punishment of the body after death. We will see that Augustine, for example, who does undertake a description of human being which integrates the body as "spouse of the soul," describes in detail the participation of the body in the eternal punishment of the unredeemed soul. Augustine's long description, in *The City of God* XXI, of how the body can burn and not be consumed, like Tertullian's graphic descriptions of vindicated Christians reveling in the spectacle of the tortured damned, finds no equivalent in Origen. When, as for Origen, the body is the condition in which the soul struggles, is "punished," and begins the long process of coming to God, then the body does not need to be punished as accomplice of the soul, but is itself already the soul's condition of punishment and learning.[94] In those Christian authors who describe the body as the unambiguously good creation of a good God, there is little sympathy for the painful insecurity of the human body. Rather, there is frequently glee in condemning it, with the soul, to eternal pain. In Origen, the body participates humbly in the effort of the soul and is finally integrated in the soul's "life and joy": "God for his part did not create human beings for ruin but for life and joy."[95]

We have seen, in Origen's metaphysical and doctrinal statements, a consistent commitment to Scriptural formulations that affirm the integrity and permanence of the body in human being. We have also seen the difficulty he had in attempting to relate this view to his speculative theology. We must not attempt to reduce this tension beyond the evidence of our texts. Origen seems to sustain a thorough-going but fruitful tension within which he thought about the meaning and value of the human body. The section of *On First Principles* in which he discusses these questions most directly ends inconclusively:

> So far, then, we have discussed the question of our bodily nature and of the spiritual body. We leave it to the reader's judgment to choose which . . . opinion he decides to be better. For our part we shall here bring the third book to a conclusion.[96]

Even when, at the end of the fourth century, Origen's speculative theology was under attack, the ascetic self-discipline for which he is famous was highly influential in eremetical and cenobitic monasticism. His rationale for asceticism has two dimensions, the freedom and responsibility of the human being, and the role of the body in the soul's learning:

> No one is stainless by essence or by nature, nor is anyone polluted essentially. Consequently it lies with us and with our own actions whether we are to be blessed and holy, or whether, through sloth and negligence we are to turn away from blessedness into wickedness and loss.[97]

"It lies with us": "our perfection does not come to pass without our doing anything, and yet it is not completed as a result of our efforts, but God performs the greater part of it."[98]

"When the body is punished the soul is purified." An indispensable method for the purification of the soul is bodily discipline. Origen does not advocate, and in fact strongly discourages, self-inflicted punish-ment. The condition of human life in the body provided plenty of occasion for self-discipline and "training" through mild ascetic practices. It may have been Origen's own youthful predilection for ascetic zeal which he calls, in his *Commentary on Matthew*,[99] "an immoderate lust for purity," which made him aware that the human being who does not respect the body's needs falls prey to the "Devil's last temptation." In despising one's own body, Origen says, Christ, who shared the condition of human embodiment, is despised. Eusebius' account of Origen's self-castration, an account which most scholars accept,[100] adds that Origen repented of this deed later, and indeed, when he exegeted the verse (Matt. 19:12), in which Jesus says that "some have made themselves eunuchs for the sake of the kingdom of heaven," Origen specifically excludes the possibility of any literal interpretation. Rather, he says, by the sword of the spirit, these "eunuchs" have cut off their sexual concupiscence without touching their body.[101] Origen himself maintained an ascetic life consistent with his principle that "it lies within our power" to effect the purification of the soul by the use of moderate ascetic practices. Eusebius reports that he lived on a minimum of food and sleep, and practiced the Gospel injunction to poverty.[102]

In summary assessment of Origen's view of the body, then, we need to account for both his maximizing of the incompatibility and distance between spirit, soul, and body, and his teaching that the body is not only the accurate reflection of the soul's condition but also the locus of the soul's education. On the one hand, we have passages in which, temporarily at least, the soul must attempt to "sever itself from the body."[103] On the other hand, in addition to suggestions that the body is the "shadow" of the soul, there is the axiom that bodily training is transferred directly to the soul. The interaction of body and soul is not one way, even though the body without the soul has no living functions. For Origen, "the medium is the message" in a very concrete way. One result of this throughout Origen's writings is his preponderant use of bodily functions and parts to describe the "inner person."

In the *Dialogue with Heraclides*, for example, Origen develops a most interesting argument for the proper understanding of such Scriptural locutions as "The soul of all flesh is blood."[104] Here Origen is at his most passionate in appealing to the spiritual sensibilities of his hearers. When we find such locutions in Scripture, he says, we must understand them to refer, not to the bodily function or part, but to its *transformed equivalent* in the "inner person." The transformation of understanding that is required anticipates and prepares for the transformation of the material body in the resurrection.[105] A long excursus relates bodily eyes to the mind's eye; bodily ears to inward ears; the "fine parts of the body—" i.e., heart, bones, and hair, and the bodily activities of taste and touch—to inward parts and activities. Origen concludes: "Thus we have all the parts of the visible body in the inner person."[106]

A further example of Origen's use of terms drawn from the body as metaphors for spiritual activities is his discussion of the highest value of human life, the vision of God, as "seeing and being seen." This discussion helps us to recognize that Origen was concerned lest we slip into confusing physical characteristics with spiritual descriptions. He tells us that we may use the locution "to see and to be seen" if we are careful to keep in mind that, in fact, "there is no existence to which God is visible; not as if he were one who is visible by nature and yet eludes and escapes the gaze of his creatures because of their frailty, but that he is in his nature impossible to be seen":

> It is one thing to see, another to know. To see and to be seen is a property of bodies; to know and to be known is an attribute of intellectual existence. Whatever therefore is proper to bodies must not be believed either of the Father or of the Son. . . . What is called "seeing" and "being seen" is, with the Father and the Son, called "knowing" and "being known," through the faculty of knowledge and not through the frail sense of sight. . . . For what else is "to see God in the heart" but to understand and know him with the mind.[107]

Origen insists that the Christian must be very conscious, when using such expressions, of the "translation" of their "corporeal significance" to a spiritual sense. It is only by consciously retaining this important distinction that they are useful. And yet, is not their usefulness more than that of metaphors? Just as in the resurrection of the body the material elements are *essentially* transformed into the glory of the spiritual body, so in understanding and appropriating the spiritual sense of Scripture corporeal locutions are transformed and integrated in the spiritual sense. This is possible only because they so accurately reflect and participate in the life of the spirit.

So Origen's view of the human body encompasses both the value and the difficulty of the body. His theology posits a body that is not eliminated in either theory or practice, but is caught up in orientation to the life in Christ. This life, which is "now present in shadow" in the human body, will, in the resurrection, include the body in "life itself." The resurrection does not discard the body, but deadness:

> The resurrection of the people that is promised is a resurrection from their fallen state, from the sort of deadness they have suffered in being handed over to their enemies through their sins. . . . It is God's part to open the grave of each of us and to bring us out of our graves, restored to life.[108]

The Christian is already, in this life, "inaccessible to death":[109] "We have passed from death to life by our transition from unbelief to faith."[110] The condition of embodiment, then, does not form a barrier to the life that transcends the human categories of life and what we usually call death.

Yet we must be careful to acknowledge that, for Origen, the role of the human body is the humble and secondary one of providing the soul with a medium in which to work and with energy for its projects. The death of the body is to be "yearned for" and "despised."[111] Even the pain of martyrdom can be anticipated with joy when the soul has converted its natural capacity to care for the body into love for God: "love for God, in the face of the most painful agonies and the severest torments, is far more powerful than any other bond of affection. This love for God and human weakness cannot dwell together in us."[112] And this view of the body influenced ascetic monasticism. Human being was seen as a hierarchy of values in which the body was both metaphysically unimportant and also, in a curious way, the place to *start*. One begins with ascetic practices that gather the body's energy for the soul's purposes, and one ends by gathering the body into the life of the resurrection.

At the moment of beginning, the soul must "despise" the body in order to concentrate on the struggle. At this stage, talk about the body is characteristically pejorative. The body is used as a foil to demonstrate the greater value of the soul. As the Christian moves closer to "perfection," that is, to a capacity for love of God which replaces "human weakness," talk about the body changes rather dramatically. When the body no longer threatens to sabotage the soul's longing for God, when the soul has begun to move toward God with confidence, the body is then described in loving affirmation as participant in the soul's quest and in its reward. We have described these moments in talk about the body as if they were temporarily distinct: first "despising" the body, and then later integrating it. But this is inaccurate. Both attitudes may appear within the same work, and apparently the author is not troubled, as we are, by such "inconsistency." This flexible esteem of the body, in the case of some authors very dramatically evident, frustrates our penchant for reducing complex ideas to a comfortable clarity.

And so traditionally we have usually opted for the pejorative interpretation. The major factor in this decision is, I think, the weight contemporary people place on human life here and now. Historic people, even up to our own time, ordered life on earth in relation to the life after death. It is enormously difficult for us to comprehend the pervasive change in values this reorientation has caused. Historic

Christians would not have recognized our predilection for living entirely in the present. The empiricism of our time pervades our consciousness to such an extent that we often forget that what seems so abundantly obvious to us was not at all obvious to historic people. The hope of a future life structured the views of historic Christians about the meaning and value of the body. If we could ourselves relive this consciousness, even briefly, it would not be difficult for us to understand the necessity for flexibility in evaluating the body. Origen is typical of other ancient authors in requiring us to experience his preoccupation with the "future life" if we are to understand his idea of the body.

III

HUMAN NATURE AND EMBODIMENT
IN AUGUSTINE

AUGUSTINE, BISHOP OF HIPPO in the North African province of Numidia at the end of the fourth century, was the first Christian author to begin his theological work with an analysis of human experience. In place of the larger-than-life cosmological speculations of Origen, Augustine began by examining the human condition and, in particular, his own human condition. In so doing, he became amazed that this method was so absent from the characteristic interests of most persons:

> And people go abroad to wonder at the heights of mountains, the huge waves of the sea, the broad streams of rivers, the vastness of the ocean, the turnings of the stars—and they do not notice themselves.[1]

Augustine began, thus, by noticing himself. In human nature as it is, he found, we observe immediately that things are not as they should be. A terrifying disjunction exists between a person's concerted efforts to be happy and the overwhelming pain of common experience. Everyone desires happiness, and yet everyone seems also instinctively to thwart those desires as quickly as they come near to fulfillment. Newly elected bishop at about the age of forty, Augustine wrote a journal in order to interpret his experience and to make it useful to those with whom he shared these *Confessions*.

Augustine told his story in a way no other late classical person did. There were other autobiographies, of course, but none began with prenatal experience. As no one before him, Augustine set his ideas in the context of his life and urged his readers to understand him and his thoughts as one. The *Confessions* present Augustine's idea of life as a strenuous learning experience. The events and circumstances that at the time he had experienced as a frenzied struggle for happiness became cumulative disillusionment that brought him to God.[2] Even the stubborn wrongfulness of his struggle for a happy life prepared for his conversion. He later wrote:

> For such as love him in this way, God makes all things work together unto good—absolutely all things, even to this extent, that if some of them swerve and stray from the path, he makes their very wanderings contribute to their good.[3]

Augustine found the roots of this struggle in concupiscence, the anxious grasping in the fear that something will be missed, at every object that crosses one's path. He saw concupiscence most clearly not in sex or even in promiscuity. His paradigm of concupiscence was the anxiety of the newborn infant, the total and painful disorientation that made the newborn the most anxious of all persons. The behavior of the infant prefigured the form of all future concupiscence. In later years the anxiety of the newborn is not eradicated but turns to new objects and with wider scope:

> For it is just these same sins which, as the years pass by, refer no longer to tutors, schoolmasters, footballs, nuts, and pet sparrows, but to magistrates and kings, gold, estates, and slaves.[4]

Concupiscence, as Augustine described it, was not technically a "sin" or "sins" but a sickness, a wound, the result of an ancient fall, and a response to the disorientation and anxiety that human beings feel as a result of this original sin. It pervades human life and motivates the struggle, extrapolated from the infant's grasping, for sex, power, and possessions. Adults learn to mask, but never to eradicate it. It is not a pleasant aspect of human experience, yet no one gives it the sympathy it deserves: "No one is sorry for the children; no one is sorry for the older people; no one is sorry for both of them."[5]

Concupiscence, according to Augustine, comes from the fact that the very essence of being human is its characteristic intentionality. Human being does not contain "the good by which it is made happy," and, therefore, the human person is characterized by his or her choice of objects by which to accomplish this.[6] The essence of personhood is this striving, this movement toward objects. Corresponding to it, there is also an intrinsic order of value, being, and goodness in creation with which one must align oneself: "You have made us for yourself, and our hearts are restless until they come to rest in you."[7] This statement epitomizes Augustine's concept of personhood as *constituted* by the object of attention and affection. This cannot be put too strongly: "For when we ask how good a person is, we do not ask what he believes or what he hopes for, but what he loves."[8] To say that one is "in relationship" with the object of one's love is inaccurate and misleading. "Relationship" implies a distance to be overcome, a gulf to be bridged. Rather, the person is connected all too intimately to what is loved, whether this be objects of physical pleasure, other human beings, or God. It will be necessary to keep in mind this idea of the person as connected by desire to the object of that desire in order to grasp Augustine's view of the body.

The "choice" of an object that is hopelessly incongruent with the intrinsic created order makes unhappiness inevitable, and, as we have seen, this wrong "choice" is made from earliest infancy:

> I panted for honors, for money, for marriage, and you were laughing at me. I found bitterness and difficulty in following these desires, and your graciousness was shown in the way you would not allow me to find anything sweet that was not you. . . . Let my soul cling to you now that you have freed it from the gripping birdlime of deadness. How unhappy it was then! And you pricked it on the quick, so that I might leave everything else and turn to you. . . . I was unhappy indeed, and you made me really see my unhappiness.[9]

Augustine saw the effects of concupiscence both in individual experience and in the general vulnerability of the human race. It is evident both in the disasters that constantly threaten human life and in the evils perpetrated by human beings. In *The City of God* XXII.21, Augustine lists the distresses of human beings, a catalog that ranges from the discipline of children to "the pains which trouble all humankind." Among these are the harshness of storm, tempest, flood, and earthquake, the terror of attacks by animals, and sudden accidents, to which "anyone walking anywhere is liable." The list includes assaults by demons, diseases for which "the treatments and medicines are themselves instruments of torture," restless dreams, "fear itself," and death.

Such clear evidence that life is disastrously out of harmony with the deep longing for happiness felt by human beings documents Augustine's analysis of the human condition as a state of punishment. To account for human existence *as it is*, Augustine made a far more detailed and emphasized use of the doctrine of original sin than any Christian author had before him.[10]

In what aspect of human being did Augustine locate this "weakness, this disease, this lethargy"?[11] The flaw, he said, lies in the will, that is, in the energy of the whole person. The will is the impetus to activity that gathers intellect and experience into action. In the original human condition, the will was intact and the motivation of the person was a delight in the intrinsically valuable object of human life. "Delight orders the soul," Augustine wrote.[12] In the original created state of human beings, delight ordered its objects not to repress "lesser" goods in favor of "greater" goods, but to ensure that *none* of the goods of being human would be neglected or lost. The first "evil act" was a falling away from this condition of a will ordered by delight. Since, for Augustine, "whatever is, is good,"[13] evil, which has no energy of its own, can only occur as a defect in human nature. And evil is in that sense "unnatural," although as a defect it can still be properly said to "belong" to human nature. It was this original sin which upset the effortless ordering by delight of human beings.

And yet Augustine was constantly amazed at the goodness and beauty that remains in human life despite its difficulties. In *City of God* XXII.24, following his catalog of pains, Augustine lists the goods remaining in the human condition. *Beginning with reproduction,* he cites "the arts and skills of humanity," the capacity of the mind, the orderliness and beauty of the body, and the blessings of the natural world. Even in the fallen condition human beings enjoy the most varied and abundant blessings:

> God, then, created all things in supreme wisdom and ordered them in perfect justice; and in establishing the mortal race of humankind as the greatest ornament of earthly things, he has given to mankind certain good things suitable to this life. These are: temporal peace, in proportion to the short span of a mortal life—the peace that consists in bodily health and soundness, and in fellowship with one's kind; and everything necessary to safeguard or recover this peace—those things, for example, which are appropriate or accessible to our senses: light, speech, air to breathe, water to drink, and whatever is suitable for the feeding and clothing of the body, for the care of the body and the adornment of the person.[14]

Augustine's diagnosis of the human condition, along with his observation that the will of some human beings is "healed" by the inscrutable grace of God, while that of others remains divided and impotent, forms the foundation of his prescription for this condition. In his account of his own conversion in *Confessions* VIII, Augustine describes himself as "suspended in hesitation."[15] The metaphor with which he describes his experience of the healing of his will is that of the child who is just beginning to walk. A voice within him says:

> Throw yourself upon him. Do not fear. He will not pull away and let you fall. Throw yourself without fear and he will receive you and heal you.[16]

This imagery implies that it is necessary to return to the earliest psychic condition of anxiety, in which the infant in terror began to grasp at objects, and to reverse that habit of concupiscence which in adulthood became settled habit:[17] "The worse part of me was stronger from habit than the better part, which was a novelty."[18] Augustine calls this inertia of habit *deadness*: "I hesitated," he wrote in *Confessions* VIII. 11, "to die to deadness and live to life"—that is, to God, of whom Augustine elsewhere wrote: "We have an absurd idea if we think of him as anything other than life itself."[19] Augustine also used the powerful imagery of infant experience to describe the restful nourishment of his healed will: "What am I at my best but an infant suckling on the milk you give and feeding upon you?"[20]

The decision to trust cannot simply be superimposed on the earlier unconscious choice—the choice of every human being through original sin, but a person must return to the terror and disorientation of the infant state to reverse it. This can no more be accomplished as an act of the divided will than could the newborn's choice have been different. Original sin permeates the human psyche at a level inaccessible to the usual methods of bribery or bullying by which human beings talk themselves into conscious choices. The will, then, must be healed, and the healing of the will consists in restoring to the human being the capacity to love. Love is the "stronger will"[21] which, overcoming the fallen divided will, enables a person to love the greatest good. The anxiety-ridden concupiscence which has ordered human existence gives place to the love of God which informs every aspect of life:

> Now Scripture enjoins nothing except love and condemns nothing except concupiscence. . . . I mean by love that affection of the mind which aims at the enjoyment of God for his own sake and of oneself and one's neighbor for God's sake. By concupiscence I mean that affection of the mind which aims at the enjoyment of oneself and one's neighbor without reference to God. . . . Now *in proportion as the dominion of concupiscence is pulled down, in the same proportion that of love is built up.*[22]

By being loved "in God," the neighbor is not devalued. Rather, the activity of love is *necessarily* participation in God who *is* love: "God, who art loved knowingly or unknowingly by everything that is capable of loving."[23] In contrast to concupiscence, in which the "neighbor" is used to reinforce and temporarily to satisfy one's grasping anxiety, loving the neighbor *in God* acknowledges the being and beauty of the neighbor in a way that is impossible to concupiscence. The curious phenomenon of a person who thinks to *make use of* the neighbor while actually *enslaved* to that use itself is one of the constant themes of the *Confessions*.[24] Even the love of oneself is possible only by participation in the love of God:

> He, therefore, who knows how to love himself, loves God; but he who does not love God, even if he loves himself—a thing implanted in him by nature—yet is not inaptly said to hate himself, inasmuch as he does that which is adverse to himself, and assails himself as though he were his own enemy.[25]

This is the basic framework of Augustine's analysis of the human condition. An accurate description of human existence—and therefore an accurate anthropology—was, if not the only preoccupation of Augustine's theology, certainly the essential factor in structuring his theological enterprise. The three major controversies in which his theology developed and matured were each concerned with understanding human existence. His polemic against the Manichaeans, which continued throughout his life,[26] focused on the affirmation of the essential goodness of the whole human person, body and soul. The Donatist controversy, with all its social and political overtones, had also to do with different versions of what can be expected of human nature and therefore with different versions of the Catholic Church, which was so notoriously a *corpus permixtum*. The Pelagian controversy also addressed the question of whether human beings can, and therefore should, be perfect. In one context or another, Augustine developed his anthropology throughout his long career.

Although he often used the Scriptural terminology of body, soul, and spirit to describe human being, his usual usage is the abbreviated body-soul locution. We will look briefly at Augustine's description of both of these parts of the human being and at his idea of the relation of body and soul. His formula, consistent throughout his life, is quite simple: "Just as the soul is the whole life of the body, so God is the blessed life of the soul."[27] A simple hierarchy appears in this formula. Augustine's interest in order, an interest that was no doubt intensified by constant threats to the political and social order in which he lived, as well as by his excitement with Platonic ideas of orderly cosmic arrangement, recommended this description to him. Although this spatial imagery of parts of the human composite stacked one upon the other came to be of far less interest to Augustine as he matured, it was a model that he never entirely relinquished. It was a truism for him that "incorporeal nature is superior to every body whatsoever."[28]

The soul, incorporeal and immortal, was the animating aspect of the human being. Without the soul, the body was quite literally a corpse. The soul's first duty, then, is to care for its body,[29] that is, to be alert to sensation, and to provide psychological motivation for the body's activities. The hierarchical scheme of human being requires, for Augustine, the conclusion that body cannot affect soul, since it is always the soul which constructs sensation with the use of its instrument, the bodily organs of sense:

> The body is not the good of the soul but rather the soul is the good of the body. For then we need no longer inquire whether that highest good or some part of it exists in the body. It is stupid to deny that the soul is better than the body. Likewise it is stupid to deny that that which bestows the blessed life or some part of it is better than that which receives it. Therefore, the soul does not receive the highest good, or any part of it, from the body.[30]

The entirely different "natures" of body and soul (*Ep.* CXXXVII) Augustine finds necessary to emphasize. We will see later some of the problems with the confusion of these two natures. The unity of body and soul was a continuing source of wonder, puzzlement, and conjecture for him. Even in discussing the incarnation of the Word, Augustine will go so far as to say that it is easier to conceive how God could become human than it is to describe how a corporeal and an incorporeal substance can form the human unity.[31] It is, in fact, a "mystery" that Augustine never claimed to have grasped or explained.

Augustine's range of ideas about the meaning and value of the human body may be classified in three major groups: he used (in the best rhetorical style) the body as a *foil* to demonstrate the greater value and beauty of the soul; he also described several ways in which the human body is a *problem*; finally, he moved more and more to the opinion that the human body is simply the *condition* of human learning, trial, and ultimate victory.

We will first examine Augustine's use of the body as foil for the soul, a rhetorical device to which Augustine was heavily inclined by his rhetorical training. This latter gave him a predilection for placing contrasting entities in juxtaposition in order to intensify description: city of God vs. city of the world, to cite one major example. Augustine did not always resist this preference for strong contrasts in discussions of body and soul. In two contexts his use of the body as foil for the soul is especially noticeable. First, in the philosophical dialogues of the period immediately after his conversion, traditional language and imagery dominate:

> There is but one thing I can teach thee; I know nothing more. These things of the senses are to be utterly shunned and the utmost care must be used lest while we bear this body our wings be impeded by their snare; seeing that we need them whole and perfect if we would fly from this darkness to that light, which deigns not even show itself to those shut up in the cage of the body unless they have been such that whether it were broken through or dissolved they would escape into air which was theirs.[32]

By the time the old Augustine wrote the *Retractions,* he regretted the use of this imagery[33] with its heavily dualistic implications. Yet the second context in which Augustine used the body as foil for the soul tones down this dualism only slightly. In the instructions Augustine gives on achieving communion with God, his language throughout his life relied on the same imagery of the need for the soul to "lift off" from the body:

> Let [the human mind] first examine and marvel at itself; let it lift itself out of the body for a little while if it can, and rise above those things which it is wont to experience through the body and let it see itself what it is that uses the body.[34]

And passages such as the following demonstrate Augustine's conviction that it is only by withdrawing energy from the body's senses that the soul can gather concentration sufficient for "seeing somewhat":

> Recognize in thyself something within, within thyself. Leave thou abroad both thy clothing and thy flesh; descend into thyself; go to thy secret chamber, thy mind. If thou be far from thine own self, how canst thou draw near unto God? For not in the body but in the mind was human being made in the image of God. In his own similitude let us seek God; in his own image recognize the Creator.[35]

Here it is a question of conservation of energy, and not necessarily a rejection of bodily senses and their objects. The soul is not itself the object of this concentration, but rather must direct its own gathered energy and attention to God, "the life of the soul":

> As the mind to the body, so must also truth be preferred to the mind itself;
> so that the mind may desire it not only more than the body, but even more
> than its own self.[36]

Yet, while elevation from the body is one of Augustine's methods for
succeeding in "seeing somewhat," it is not his only method. In the
following passage Augustine expertly combines his favored method of a
cyclic relationship with the sensible world, and what he calls "sensible
contact with God."[37]

> But yet, when I love thee, what is it that I love? Not the beauty of any
> body, not the order of time, not the clearness of this light that so gladdens
> our eyes, not the harmony of sweet songs of every kind, not the fragrance
> of flowers, or spice of aromatical odors, not manna, not honey, not limbs
> delightful to the embrace of flesh and blood. Not these things do I love in
> loving my God. Yet do I love a kind of light, a kind of voice, a kind of odor,
> a kind of food, a kind of embracing, when I love my God, who is the light,
> the voice, the odor, the food, the embracing of my inward person; when
> that light shineth into my soul which is not circumscribed by any place;
> when that voice soundeth which is not snatched away by time, when that
> odor pours forth which is not scattered by the air, when that food savours
> the taste which is unconsumed by eating, when that embracement is
> enjoyed which is not divorced by satiety. This it is which I love when I
> love my God.[38]

One is not to reject physical things, but to "accustom oneself to find in
corporeal things the traces of spiritual things that . . . one may reach the
unchangeable truth itself through which these things have been
made."[39] Of Augustine's two most prominent uses of the body as foil for
the soul, then, one is modified by his own later rejection of it, and the
other, the instruction for mystical experience, is modified by a careful
analysis of the soul's withdrawal from the sinner as only *one moment*, and
that a preliminary one, in the process of mystical communion.

Secondly, Augustine's descriptions of the human body as a problem
exhibit a great wealth of imagery. But it is important to understand the
precise sense in which the body is a problem in order not to confuse this
imagery with that employed in describing the body as foil for the soul.
We will look at the several different ways Augustine finds the human
body a problem.

> But among all the things which are possessed in this life, by God's most
> just laws and on account of the ancient sin, the body is human being's
> heaviest bond. *Nothing must be proclaimed more openly and understood*

more secretly. Lest this bond be shaken and scattered, it disturbs the soul with the fear of toil and grief; and lest it be removed and destroyed, it disturbs the soul with the fear of death. For, through force of habit, the soul loves the body, without understanding that, if it uses the body well and knowledgeably, its resurrection and renewal will, by divine law and work, be made subject to its authority without any antipathy. But when the soul turns wholly to God with this love, these things are understood.[40]

Augustine, as has been described, did not find the pain and difficulty of human life a "natural" condition. He was so deeply impressed by the immensity and ubiquity of human suffering that only an explanation that located the cause of this suffering outside ordinary human experience could begin to account for it:

Although we do not want it, our soul is often disturbed, our flesh knows pain, grows old and dies, and we suffer in many other ways. We would not suffer against our will if our nature were to obey our will in every way and in all its parts. But *the flesh experienced something because of which it is not allowed to serve.* What does it matter how it happens, as long as, through the justice of the Lord God, whom we did not willingly and submissively serve, our flesh, which had been submissive to us, has become harmful to us by not serving us? . . . And so *what we have received is our punishment.*[41]

Human life is unintelligible without the assumption that the gratuitous suffering of humankind is a punishment: "What else is the message of all the evils of humanity?"[42] The only conclusion to be drawn, for example, from the sufferings of little children is that "it may be made especially clear to us that this life is a calamity to be deplored, while the other is the felicity for which we should yearn."[43] Not only does the constant vulnerability to distress and disaster imply a state of punishment, but death, "the last enemy," receives a far less minimizing interpretation by Augustine than we have yet seen elsewhere. Death is, quite simply, the "cross we have to bear":

For our cross which the Lord bids us carry to the end that we may follow him with the least impediment, what is it but the mortality of our flesh?[44]

In marked contrast to the statements about "despising" death in earlier Christian authors, Augustine presents the necessity of death in a completely different light. To his own question: "Is death, which separates soul and body, really a good thing for the good?" Augustine answers: "The death of the body, the separation of the soul from the body, is not good for anyone. . . . It is a harsh and unnatural experience."[45]

The two aspects of the human condition, then, which, from Augustine's careful observation and analysis of his own experience, most strenuously indicate that human life has an irreducible aspect of punishment about it, are death and concupiscence. Concupiscence is the insubordination of the soul which, by claiming the ability to break its connection to its creator, forfeits the integrated "obedience" of the body.[46] The body is not responsible for concupiscence; it is its "helpless victim." The body is *sinned against* by the concupiscence of the soul.

But the soul is also vulnerable to the body. The soul, which must "conduct everything through its own body,"[47] "only partly possesses" the body on whose instrumentality it is so dependent:

> But human nature in him was vitiated and altered, so that he experienced the rebellion and disobedience of desire in his body, and was bound by the necessity of dying.[48]

Death and concupiscence are the evidence of the state of "punishment" in which human life suffers, and the body is implicated in both. Augustine was poignantly aware of the "race towards death in which no one is allowed the slightest pause or any slackening of the pace."

> There is no one, it goes without saying, who is not nearer to death this year than he was last year, nearer tomorrow than today, today than yesterday, who will not by and by be nearer than he is at the moment, or is not nearer at the present time than he was a little while ago.[49]

But concupiscence is an even more ubiquitous reminder of the soul's vulnerability to the body. The problem of human life is the uneasiness with which soul and body, so different in nature, cohabit. The soul, "loving its own power, slips from what is whole and common to what is partial and private."[50] Now there is a sense in which what is the "soul's own" most immediately is the body. The soul, then, delights in "corporeal forms and movements; . . . *the soul is wrapped in their images*, which it has fixed in memory";[51] it is "given over to the bodily senses" or "immersed" in physical pleasure. The problem is not—emphatically not—either the bodily senses themselves or physical pleasure. It is the condition of being addicted—enslaved, to use Augustine's word—to these pleasures.

When the soul, with its innate intentionality, identifies itself with the body, it takes on the bodily potential to habituation and fatigue, so that objects which once gave pleasure do not continue to do so. The person, then, cannot *rest* in them, but in order to experience the same pleasure one experienced the first time, must constantly increase the dosage. One becomes enslaved: "loving these things, human beings become subject to them, and subjects cannot judge."[52] The anxious pursuit of pleasures—in young adulthood sublimated into the quest for "honors, money, and marriage"—of Augustine's self-description emphasizes this theme:

> I was toiling away, spurred on by my desires and dragging after me the load of my unhappiness. . . . I got no joy out of my learning. . . . I was eaten up with anxieties. . . . How we hated the whole wearisome business of human life. . . . What torturous ways these were, and how hopeless was the plight of my foolhardy soul, which hoped to have something better if it went away from you! It has turned indeed, over and over, on back and side and front, and always the bed was hard and you alone are rest.[53]

The most characteristic feature of the bodily senses is a tendency to habituation. Even when the soul has learned to "withdraw into itself," the close and loving association with its body inevitably marks the soul's experience. Even in the strongest experiences of communion with God, the person, because of "the habit of the body," falls away from the "trembling glance" to "habitual ways":

> Even if, by walking in desire, we manage somehow or other to dispel the clouds and to reach up to those sounds at times, and succeed by straining our ears in catching something from that house of God; yet under the burden of our weakness we fall back again to the humdrum things we are used to.[54]

The problem of the body is abundantly obvious—and well and continuously documented—in the experience of every human being. But it is not, Augustine says, perfectly accurate to say that it is the human body that inhibits, disciplines, and burdens the soul:

> It is not the body as such, but the corruptible body, that is a burden to the soul. Hence the Scriptural statement, . . . "The corruptible body weighs down the soul." The addition of "corruptible" shows that the writer meant that the soul was weighed down, not by any kind of body, but by the body as it became as a result of sin and the punishment that followed.[55]

Although Augustine saw the dangers and distresses to which human beings are vulnerable as a kind of "punishment," he objected to the late classical commonplace of referring to the body as a prison. Such language implicitly denied that the body was an integral part of the

human being, something Augustine found incompatible with the
Christian affirmation of the whole person:

> You consider the flesh as fetters, but who loves his fetters? You consider
> the flesh a prison, but who loves his prison? . . . No matter how great a
> master of the flesh you may be, and no matter how great may be the
> severity toward the flesh with which you are kindled, I am inclined to
> think that you will close your eye if any blow threatens it.[56]

Augustine also saw hypocrisy behind the claim that the body was to be
despised. He used Eph. 5:29 again and again as an example of
spontaneous love:

> Neither does anyone hate his own body. For the apostle truly said, "No
> one ever hated his own flesh." And when some say that they would rather
> be without a body altogether, they entirely deceive themselves. For it is
> not their body but its heaviness and corruption which they hate. And so it
> is not no body, but an uncorrupted and very light body that they want.[57]

Thirdly, Augustine regarded the human body as the *condition* of the
soul's learning, trial, and reward. The incarnation of Christ was the
paradigm of the meaning and value of embodiment:

> It is said, "The flesh profiteth nothing," . . . but this means to itself. Let
> the spirit be added to the flesh, as love is added to knowledge, and it
> profiteth much. For if the flesh profiteth nothing, the Word had not been
> made flesh that it might dwell in us. If through the flesh Christ hath
> greatly profited us, how does the flesh profit nothing? But it is through the
> flesh that the spirit acted for our salvation. . . . For how could the sound
> of the Word reach us except through the flesh?[58]

Not only is the human body the condition of the soul's trial and
learning on earth, but it is also the condition of its resurrection to eternal
life. Only in the resurrection is the uneasy cohabitation of body and soul
to be fully overcome, and then the body will be permanently and
completely integrated. The reward of the human struggle and the gift of
grace will thus be a *bodily* experience:

> And in case anyone should still suppose that it is not what is buried that is
> to rise again but that it is as if one garment is laid aside and a better one
> taken instead, he [the apostle] proceeds to show distinctly that the same
> body will be changed for the better, as the garments of Christ in the
> mount were *not displaced but transfigured.* . . . And if it should be said
> that it is not as regards our mortal and corruptible body, but as regards our
> soul, that we are to be changed, it should be observed that the apostle is
> not speaking of the soul, but of the body.[59]

Even the bodily eyes will, Augustine says, probably "see God." In an about-face from his own earlier view that the claim to see God with the eyes of the body was "insane,"[60] Augustine in his later years described a heaven almost embarrassingly concrete:

> It is possible, indeed most probable, that we shall then see the physical bodies of the new heaven and the new earth in such a fashion as to observe God in utter clarity and distinctness, seeing him present everywhere and governing the whole material scheme of things by means of the bodies we shall then inhabit and the bodies we shall see wherever we turn our eyes.[61]

But "we do not yet see,"[62] Augustine insisted. Although he used the classical description of the "vision" of God to describe the experiences of communion that occur in this life, he found the metaphor of vision not quite accurate for the human condition and often preferred to use the metaphor of hearing to capture the constructed picture of truth to which human beings have access. In the passage from Psalm 41 quoted above,[63] Augustine's description of "seeing somewhat" is curiously nonvisual. "If," he wrote, "we manage somehow or other to . . . reach up to those sounds . . . and succeed by straining our ears to catch something from the house of God, yet under the burden of our weakness we fall back again to the humdrum things we are used to."[64] The sacrifice Augustine makes in order to anticipate a fully human experience in which all the difficulties, obstacles, and pain of present experience are overcome is that of postponing this experience beyond our present conditions of time and space. It we are not willing to entertain what this sacrifice might mean, we will not understand Augustine's idea of the body; both his emphasis on the painfulness and vulnerability of the body and his ecstatic description of the bodily experience of the resurrection will strike us as exaggerated and rhetorical. It is clear that Augustine polarized the conditions of bodily experience in order to direct the energy of longing to the resurrection experience and to foster an attitude of acceptance with regard to the "necessities" of our present experience.

To the same degree that embodiment is painfully tinged with anxiety, vulnerability, and pain—a "punishment"—the resurrection of the body will beatify physical experience by relieving it of the inevitable neediness of human life.

> If I were to say that the body would rise again to be hungry and thirsty, to be sick and to suffer, to be subject to corruption, you would be right in refusing to believe me. . . . The flesh will rise incorruptible; the flesh will

rise without defect, without blemish, without mortality, without burden, and without weight. *What now brings pain to you will then be your glory.*[65]

We will look, in the concluding section of this book, at Augustine's idea of the function of ascetic practices. For now it is enough to observe that one of his central interests is that of "keeping body and soul together" as much as possible until the resurrection, when the whole human being will enjoy eternal life. In the present life, Augustine's agenda is to move one from contempt of one's body as subordinate to the soul's habitual concupiscence to love for it as the body of the resurrection. This language strikes us as curiously contemporary, but it is Augustine's own:

> Human beings must be instructed, therefore, about the manner of loving, that is, how they ought to love themselves so that they may help themselves. . . . They must be instructed how to love their bodies that they may take care of them reasonably and wisely. . . . If you consider yourself in your entirety, your soul and body (for human beings are composed of soul and body), and your neighbor in his entirety, his soul and body, . . . no class of objects to be loved has been omitted in these two commandments.[66]

Just as the relationship of the human to the physical world and to other human beings must change from one of concupiscence to one of love, so one's body must be no longer regarded as a tool of the soul's pursuit of sex, power, and possessions. These passions, as Augustine says, "have a bad effect on the body."[67] Rather, one's body is to be lovingly regarded as the "spouse of the soul,"[68] the permanent and integral partner of the soul in delight in the good:

> Is not our absorbing love of life really the soul's love for its body, a love which will haunt it until that body is returned to it risen and glorious?[69]

We should not conclude this discussion of Augustine's view of the human body without mentioning his views on sexuality.[70] The Augustine we have heard most about is the Augustine of the *Confessions* in his conversion to celibacy. And it is also the old Augustine of the controversy with Julian whose views on sex seem to us as negative as they were influential. How are Augustine's view that the body is the "spouse" of the soul and his insistence that the body is an essential and permanent aspect of human being to be reconciled with his unequivocal statement to Julian that even though sex is redeemed by the good of children that come from it, "the action is not performed without evil"?[71]

In the *Confessions*, as we have said, Augustine urged his readers to understand his ideas in the context of his life, and they have not often done this. He himself pointed out the inadequacy of proof-texting without regard for context:

> Do not be crafty in using one group of testimonies of sacred Scripture and remaining deaf to the other, and you will be converted in both. For, if you accept these latter as they deserve, you will try to understand the former, also, in their truth.[72]

Not only modern commentators but also medieval followers of Augustine have ignored the overwhelming contextual evidence of his struggle to integrate the body and to understand the implications of embodied experience. In order more adequately to understand this context, we must accept Augustine's evaluation of himself as addicted to sex, from which, he tells us, no friendship was free.[73] It is fashionable to smile at Augustine's adolescent foibles as normal teenaged behavior, but to do so is to ignore his feeling that sex dominated and *ordered* his life. Even if we had more concrete details of Augustine's sexual behavior, we could make no more accurate evaluation. Augustine knew himself to be addicted to sex, and the resolution of this by the decision for celibacy was not a solution that he urged for anyone else not similarly addicted. His decision was a "gift of God," not the result of repression. He never tells us it was hard to maintain this state, but only that he found it tremendously freeing. Celibacy was certainly, for Augustine, the "better way," but even in his treatise on continence he was careful to acknowledge the personal nature of it, and his treatise on marriage describes the inadequacy of valuing objective "goods" without reference to their usefulness in the lives of persons:

> It is not right to compare persons with persons in some one good. For it can happen that one does not have something that the other has, but he has something that is to be valued more highly. [For example:] Greater, indeed, is obedience than the good of continence.[74]

Yet, resolved as he is to speak from his own experience, Augustine cannot resist saying that "in no way can it be doubted that the chastity of continence is better than the chastity of marriage."[75]

Augustine's statement about the unavoidability of concupiscence in every sexual act, in the controversy with Julian, should likewise not be taken out of context. His concern there was not to locate an "evil" of human life in a particular act, but to recognize and acknowledge its presence in all human activities. Julian denied its existence in married sex, so Augustine insisted on it *even* there. We can imagine that if the controversy with Julian had lighted on the question of whether power or possessions were an unambiguous "good," Augustine might have insisted in the same way—and in nearly identical statements—on the element of concupiscence involved in these cases. We know, in fact, from Augustine's letters, that he was also concerned with the relation of concupiscence to power and possessions. Yet isolating his statements on sex can make his difficulties with it seem the only preoccupation of his theological and pastoral work. This is far from the case, as his strongly affirmative statements about the human body clearly show. Augustine was *interested* in the human body. He saw that Christian authors had not integrated their view of the body with their affirmation of the fully human incarnation of the Word and their insistence on resurrection of the body, and he set out to remedy this. Without glossing over the problems of human embodiment, he attempted to describe the body's participation in the suffering, beauty, and pathos of this life, and its ultimate participation in the resurrection. Like all of us, Augustine was partially thwarted by his personal predilections and cultural assumptions, but this should not obscure the immensity of the task he set for himself, the skill and commitment with which he worked on it, or the value of his achievement—the description of the integrity and continuity of embodied experience:

> There where the greatest peace will prevail, nothing will be unsightly, nothing inharmonious, nothing monstrous, nothing to offend the eyes, but in all things God will be praised. For if now, in such frailty of the flesh and in such weak operation of our members, such great beauty of the body appears that it entices the passionate and stimulates the learned and the thoughtful to investigate it, . . . how much more beautiful will the body be there, where there will be . . . no corruption, no unsightly deformity, no miserable necessity, but instead, unending eternity, and beautiful truth, and the utmost happiness?[76]

IV

EAST AND WEST
AFTER AUGUSTINE

I

WE TURN NOW from looking at the theological ideas and texts of *individuals* who wrote about their ideas of the body to consider a period when theological ideas were less the product of individuals than the popular appropriation of Christian ideas as forms of piety. Whether or not we think medieval popular piety accurately understood the theological concerns of the classical world, it represented a vigorous appropriation of ideas of the incarnation of the Word and of the resurrection of the body. We must remember that miracles and saints were not solely the fascination of uneducated barbarians and rustics, but were an excitement shared by educated and uneducated, rich and poor, women and men alike. Medieval people remind us that theological ideas are not always—and perhaps not even usually—worked out in the cloistered studies of monastic or academic theologians! The Christian ideas that whole societies found useful for understanding and conducting their lives should command our respectful attention.

The Christian thinkers considered thus far have shared large parts of the world view of classical thought. For them, the Christian doctrines of the incarnation of the Word and the resurrection of the body presented difficulties that demanded resolution and explanation. The human body had for them a variable value depending on whether they were discussing the body as entered, redeemed, and resurrected by Christ, or whether they were giving instructions about the need to gather, focus, and direct energy toward God and away from physical existence. Origen, for example, places the body midway between "spirit" and "flesh," the pawn of a struggle for possession. In its cosmic setting, human being occupies a place between—and connected with—the "one original principle" and the material world. Its parts, sometimes described as body and soul, and sometimes as body, soul, and spirit, are arranged hierarchically; they reflect and participate in the cosmic hierarchy, with matter as lowest, and the purely spiritual originating principle as highest. It is important to notice, in this hierarchical description, the strong connection of each part to the part immediately higher and the part immediately lower. Human being defines itself by strengthening one of these connections, inevitably at the expense of the other. If the energy of the soul's attention and affection flows toward the body, physical pleasures and material comforts, then the connection to the life of the spirit and to God is neglected. If, on the other hand, the soul's longing moves upward to strengthen the connection to God, the body is ultimately carried with the soul's momentum toward the immortality that Augustine describes as "perfect health of body."[1] In late classical Christian authors, this hierarchical anthropological model was used to emphasize both the need to convert the soul's energy to its "upper connection" and also to emphasize the way in which the body shares the soul's participation in the life of Christ. Both affirmation of the integration of the body, talk about "despising" the body (as we now know it), and welcoming its death can thus derive from the hierarchical view of human being.

In the work of Augustine a new emphasis on the natural world and on the body as the location of concrete visible evidence of God's direct activity began to emerge. Without jettisoning the hierarchical anthropology, Augustine worked with doctrinal understandings that required a more explicit description of the integration of the body in the full range of human experience, including present embodied experience. An interesting indication of this concern was Augustine's altered view of the purpose and value of miracles. In his early work, *De vera religione,* he said that miracles no longer occurred as they had in the early church because these were necessary only in a time when people needed instant dramatizations of the efficacy of Christian faith.[2] Now that people can *reason* to Christian faith, miracles are no longer required. But by the time, toward the end of his life, that he wrote Book XXII of the *City of God,* Augustine was collecting, verifying, and publishing accounts of miracles as the sign of God's direct activity in the concrete world of events and bodies.[3] Augustine's interest in miracles is not a concession to popular credulity but rather the wave of the future, in which both educated and uneducated people would share the excitement of evidences of God's power in the sensible world.

Augustine was certainly not alone in his attempt to describe the meaning of the incarnation of Christ. We have seen that the Christian doctrines that place embodiment firmly at the center of human experience were those which Christian authors had to defend most persistently against the attacks of pagans and Gnostics. The doctrine, normative for Christian belief, of the coming of God to the physical world in full human embodiment, alarmed and enraged classical intellects. Their intellectual world posited a hierarchical participation of the entire cosmos in the divinity of its origin, but they could not imagine or accept the sort of collapse of the intimately connected dynamic hierarchy of being which could allow the original principle abruptly to enter the material world. I will call this view of the shortcut made possible by identifying with Christ, who gathered in himself the whole cosmic hierarchy from highest to lowest, the incarnational view.[4] Christian authors recognized only gradually the difficulty of conflating the hierarchical and the incarnational views. The trinitarian disputes were the beginning of this realization. The trinitarian disputes were the struggle of the hierarchical cosmic view with the affirmation—unintelligible to the classical intellect—that two entities, one of which was generated from the other, could occupy an equal position at the top of the cosmic hierarchy. The Christological controversies thrashed out in the metaphysical dimension a description of the incarnation which affirmed that Christ fully integrated God and human being. Trinitarian teachings such as that of Arius, and apparently also Origen, sought to conflate hierarchical and incarnational views by a subordinationist description of the place of the second person of the Trinity. The violence of these struggles indicates the magnitude of the difficulty, which must be understood as no less than a Copernican revolution, with all its implications of unsettling and disorienting psychological change.

It was the orderliness of the universe which delighted and dazzled classical people, an order in which every stage of the hierarchy reflected those above. In this orderly cosmos, human beings, by identifying with the immediately higher part of their own nature, could ascend in a graded series of stages or steps to awareness of the originating principle of the universe. Plotinus described the progress in which the life energy of the individual soul can be gathered in conscious participation in the cosmic soul; from there one can move to the intellectual plane, advancing in stability and lifefulness.[5] One then waits for the vision of the One whose creative energy informs the entire process. The hierarchical arrangement is both permeable and dynamic.

This description of the cosmic situation and task of human beings was not rejected by Christian writers but was amended in fundamental ways. Elements of the hierarchical view were preserved and more or less adequately integrated with an incarnational view, but the center of interest of the incarnational view is very different. By the sixth century, people were no longer fascinated by the orderly and trustworthy hierarchical arrangement of human being and the cosmos, but rather by the way in which the incarnation acted as a model of the activity of God in the sensible world. In the incarnational view, the unexpected and unpredictable activity of God within the material world was seen as the result of a new relationship of the highest and lowest entities of the cosmic hierarchy which was brought about by the bonding of these levels in the incarnation of the Word. Sensitized by a century of debate over the exact relationship of human and divine in Christ, people came gradually to ask themselves what could now be expected of the material and sensible world because of God's newly intimate participation in it in the incarnation. No longer was an experience of God available only to those with the time and leisure to organize their lives around contemplation, but everyone could anticipate sensible evidence of the sudden irruption of God's power in miracles. In the incarnation, God had chosen a new form of expression that made an experience of God's activity accessible to ordinary people. Because of the incarnation the power of God could be anticipated as acting in the material world in spontaneous, unpredictable, and gratuitous flashes of power.

But just as the incarnation was a concentrated and localized irruption of God in time and space, so the miraculous does not occur either erratically or evenly in the sensible world. The sanctity of particular living or dead human beings, of particular places, and of particular objects, acts like a lightning rod to collect and communicate God's power. Moreover, just as the sudden integration of God and the material world in the incarnation abbreviated or short-cut the slow ascent to God of the hierarchical view, the collapse of the "highest" and "lowest" aspects of human being meant that the sanctity achieved by the soul could be expected to appear in tangible physical or material evidence. Soul and body in saintly human beings had a similarly intimate relationship, so that the achievement of the soul could be immediately validated by the saint's power over bodies and objects. We will look more closely at the relationship of sanctity and power in the writings of several early medieval writers. But we must first pause to take notice of the social situation in which these ideas developed and were useful.

At the same time that one needs to acknowledge the deterioration of the Roman bureaucracy and of classical learning deplored by early medieval people like Gregory of Tours, we need also to recognize the fruitfulness of that medieval period. Historians like W. C. Bark demonstrate, against the now-traditional picture of "decline and fall," that the sixth century witnessed the greatest technological innovation until the twentieth century.[6] The collapse of the Roman Empire was also that of an antiquated bureaucratic machinery that required a disproportionate and exhausting amount of upkeep compared to the services it performed. Just as Augustine had argued that it was not the gods that had protected Rome but Rome that had protected the gods, so Bark pictures a Roman bureaucracy that did not so much provide a milieu in which human beings could flourish as it required people to use their energies uncreatively to maintain the machinery of government and war: "Medieval society was functional in ways that had not been dreamed of in classical civilization."[7] "What people of that time actually did was to strike out in new directions in search of new solutions to problems found unsolvable in the Greco-Roman west of ancient times."[8] Inventions and new uses of old inventions, such as the breast collar for horses, the three-field system, the waterwheel, and the shoeing of horses, were innovative responses to the needs and capacities of an agrarian society.

This picture is important for us if we are to understand the practical and creative energy of early medieval people. The theological interests of the sixth, seventh, and eighth centuries show an analogous practical creativity. The unanimity of historians—following Gibbon—that this period should be seen as a time of deterioration and decay has made it impossible for us to understand that medieval people approached theological interpretation in the same lively and innovative way that they approached the practical problems of their agrarian existence.

The new status of the physical world was evident in the excitement over pilgrimage to the "Holy Land," the scene of Christ's incarnation. At the end of the fourth century the nun Egeria described a liturgy oriented around the very spots that witnessed the events of Christ's life and passion. The urge to put one's body *on the spot*, to experience and benefit from the *virtus* or energy accessible through a physical location, to participate in a liturgy which is an orchestration of this experience: these were the fascinations of a large number of pilgrims at the end of the fourth century. Egeria emphasized the stational location of the Easter week services and the representational drama that depicted the passion events. Holy Week began with the Palm Sunday reenactment of Christ's entry into Jerusalem, the bishop playing the part of Christ. Holy Thursday featured an all-night vigil at the stations on the Mount of Olives, followed by a vivid enactment of the scene of Christ's arrest that was accompanied by loud moaning and groaning of the crowds of people participating in these services.

Another evidence of the new status of the physical world can be seen in the definition of the exact nature of the participation of God in the material form of the Eucharistic elements, which Cyril of Alexandria describes. A significant modification of the early Christian emphasis on the Eucharist as the thanksgiving service of the worshiping community appears in Cyril's work. The unquestioned Eucharistic theology at the beginning of the fifth century emphasized transformation of the Eucharistic elements into the body and blood of Christ. Cyril's interpretation—a gloss on John 6: "Unless you eat the flesh of the Son of man and drink his blood, you have no life in you"—is not unprecedented,[9] but in this description there is a new concreteness in the use of images to highlight the material aspect of the Eucharistic elements. These elements are themselves the life-giving aspect of the celebration: "Christ as God makes us alive, not merely by granting us a share in the Holy Spirit, but by granting us in edible form the flesh which he assumed."[10]

The concern of the early Christians over access to and participation in the "true life" of Christ had centered around the mediation of this life by the community in the activity of thankful recognition of the gift of this life. Cyril's emphasis is on the reception of the "true life" by ingesting the Eucharist. The life of Christ is incarnate in physical elements. In the act of eating and drinking, the recipient is transformed and deified: "Christ dyed the soul of human beings with the stability and unchangeability of his own nature . . . as wool is embued with a dye."[11] It was Cyril's understanding of the incarnation as a complete bonding of the nature of the Word and human nature that informed this description of the material elements of the Eucharist as containing and communicating Christ's life. A strong synthesis of divinity and the material world in the incarnation is the basis of Cyril's Eucharistic doctrine: the incarnation is the paradigm of the Eucharistic celebration.

What many historians of medieval culture and doctrine have called a "system of superstition"[12] can be seen much more accurately and fruitfully as the translation into practical expression of the concern of the

Trinitarian and Christological controversies of an earlier time, namely, the definition of what people can expect to experience because of the new relationship of God and matter. The incarnational view of human being and the cosmos was translated by early medieval people into concrete, experiential terms. Often the hierarchical view of classical culture was superimposed on the incarnational view. We will see some of the implications of the conflating of these two views of the world and humanity. The orderly cosmos of the hierarchical view had been reflected by the classical order. In the medieval period, the disorderliness of society became the model for a revised picture of the cosmos that accorded much more happily with the incarnational view in which both the forces of evil and the ultimately more powerful activity of God struggle in the sensible world. Evil was no longer understood as the inertia of unformed matter but as a force that can temporarily challenge God's power. We see in the lamentations of the Roman consul Boethius the bewilderment of a person caught between the no longer persuasive hierarchical view and the not yet fully understood incarnational view. Boethius, unjustly imprisoned—according to his report—by the Ostrogothic ruler Theodoric in the first quarter of the sixth century, manifests the disorientation of a highly educated classical thinker from a world that no longer could be interpreted as an orderly reflection of cosmic hierarchy:

> I am not so discouraged by what has happened to me that I complain now of the attacks of evil men against virtue; the reason for my surprise is that they have accomplished what they set out to do. The desire to do evil may be due to human weakness; but for the wicked to overcome the innocent in the sight of God—this is monstrous.[13]

Boethius holds the hierarchical notion that evil is "nothing." His settled conviction of a universe in which virtue, happiness, and the good are identified and in which misfortune is trustworthy, either as "testing virtue" or as "correcting and punishing vice," has failed in a world where "the wicked accomplish what they set out to do." Boethius died in A.D. 524; by the time of the death of Gregory the Great in 604, a cultivated Roman Christian and civic leader will be able to accept and explain the disorderliness of society as the arena of a cosmic struggle between God and evil, the reflection of a spontaneous cosmos in which God upset human expectations by appearing in the material world in human flesh.

It is in this context that we need to understand the interest in miracles, saints, and relics of Western medieval people who were as dissimilar as the scholarly monk, Bede "venerabilis," the aristocratic civic leader, Gregory I "the Great," and the semibarbarian provincial bishop, Gregory of Tours, whose Latin, he disarmingly tells us, was atrocious.

In the *History of the Franks,* Gregory, bishop of Tours, describes the preoccupation of early medieval people with *virtus,* the capacity of holy people, places, and material objects to contain and transmit healing of all sorts by physical proximity. Gregory presents a lively picture of society and popular piety in his time. We see people who were fascinated by powerful energy and by the capacity of the senses to recognize the activity of God in changes in society and the natural world. The theological niceties of a century earlier have been foreshortened in Gregory to a practical concern and excitement with what *works,* with demonstrations of God's power. We may consider this interest limited, but we should remember that it was a correction of the abstract theological interests of the controversies in the direction of usefulness to the real lives of human beings. New medieval societies developed new theological interests along with new styles of organizations and new leaders. Gregory's description of Clovis, for example, focuses on the *virtus* by which Clovis conquered and ruled. Gregory's distance from Boethius can readily be seen in his facile assumption that Clovis' *virtus* must indicate *sanctus,* or holiness. While Boethius could recognize and acknowledge that these qualities were diverging in the society of his time, Gregory insists on identifying them with each other at all costs. Describing Clovis' ruthless slaughter of his neighbors and appropriation of their territories, Gregory writes:

> When they [the neighboring kings] were dead, Clovis received all their kingdoms and treasures; and having killed many other kings and his nearest relatives, of whom he was jealous lest they take the kingdom from him, he extended his rule over all the Gauls.

He further proceeds blandly to announce:

> For God was laying his enemies low every day under his hand, and was increasing his kingdom, because he walked with an upright heart before him, and did what was pleasing in his sight.[14]

Associated with this interest in power is a harsh asceticism that often bears the unmistakable flavor of the theatrical. Medieval people tended

to identify sanctity with *virtus* so that they expected that a person with
great power was holy, as we have seen in Gregory's account of Clovis, or
conversely, that a person of unmistakable holiness had power. The
incarnational view shows its characteristic temptation to identify power
and holiness at this point. In the hierarchical scheme, the body occupies
the lowest position both metaphysically and practically. But in the
incarnational view, the body assumes an ambiguous importance.
Dramatic abuse of the body certified holiness, but curiously, the reward
of this holiness was expected to be some form of bodily benefit as well as
less concretely defined spiritual healing. The hierarchical position of the
body has been conflated with this ambiguous esteem and attention to it,
both as a source of vitality that can be used for the spiritual life, and as the
locus of reward. But the power that medieval people accumulated by the
practice of severe forms of asceticism was not only spiritual, it was also
highly social. Such extreme practices as immuring—in which an ascetic,
at his or her own request, is placed in a narrow cell and the walls closed
so that only a slim hole remains through which to pass minimal portions
of food—attracted great attention. The validity of this practice, either for
the spiritual benefit of the practitioner or for the benefit of others, must
have been negligible, and Gregory does not attempt to describe it. He
even reports a case of predictable madness as the result of
immurement.[15] But apparently the self-confinement of the ascetic did
not prevent him from becoming the object of interest and the bearer of
impressive political power. "Recluses" foretold barbarian invasions,
counseled and warned people of their sins, and gave practical advice
about how to fortify towns against the barbarians.

The more dramatic ascetic practices tend to attract us just as they
attracted medieval people, and so we often neglect to notice that it was
also the simple but heroic goodness of ordinary persons which Gregory
found important to relate. *Sanctus* could manifest itself in very humble
and touching ways. He tells, for example, of a parish priest who, when
plague was raging, "never left the place, but remained courageously
burying the people and celebrating mass. He was a priest of great
kindness," Gregory concludes, "and friend of the poor."[16] Most of the
saints Gregory describes are extraordinarily practical. One recluse,
Ebarchius, renowned for his devoutness, specialized in driving demons
from the bodies they possessed, cured pimples, and "often rather
ordered than requested judges to spare the guilty. For he was so
attractive in his address that they could not deny him when he asked a
favor." One prisoner, clearly guilty of numerous thefts and murders,

was pleaded for by Ebarchius to no avail. The people of the region demanded his execution for their own safety, and the judge could not deny the reasonableness of their request. The prisoner was executed, and Ebarchius had to content himself with bringing the condemned man back to life after the execution.[17] Presumably his punishment had an edifying effect on the prisoner so that he amended his life, but Gregory does not report this!

Miracles that restore social order or physical health predominate in the *History of the Franks*. Gregory's miracle accounts give us a sense of everyday quality. In the harsh world of his time, in which mothers would attempt to strangle daughters, wives kill husbands with poison, and old friends stab each other in sudden drunken rages, many things we would account for as coincidence or "good luck" must have seemed miraculous: a headache getting better, a sudden change of heart in a vengeful person, the turning of a plague, the escape of a prisoner, and so on. There is, in Gregory's account, very little middle ground for the ordinary; every event is intensified into the miraculous or the diabolical. Medieval people looked everywhere for God's power, and they found it everywhere.

But even witnessing a miracle was often itself a mark of sanctity, since not everyone present at the occurrence of a miracle recognized it. Holier persons can more readily identify miracles. Gregory tells of an adulterous deacon from whose hand the monstrance flew to the altar, not allowing itself to be touched by someone unworthy. Gregory says, "It was granted only to one priest and three women . . . to see this; the rest did not see it. I was present, I confess . . . but I had not the merit to see this miracle."[18] Miracles were always marked by a psychological response of joyful amazement. This response, frequently noted in miracle accounts, was the subjective equivalent of the objective event. If it were missing, there would be no "miracle."

Medieval people were not unaware of the borderline character of the miraculous. Gregory complains of the inaccessibility of many miracles, both because of the difficulty of identifying and observing them, and because many of those to whom they occurred preferred to remain anonymous: "When they are restored to health by the saint of God, they leave immediately, and they sometimes go so secretly that . . . they are noticed by no one."[19] Gregory, who would have liked to appropriate for his churches the publicity of these miracles, was frustrated. He knew that miracle accounts not accompanied by facts tended to be considered "unworthy of belief."

The *virtus* which accompanies holiness, then, can locate in places: the scene of the death of saints or their tombs, material objects, the bones of saints and martyrs, or persons of unusual spiritual power. Gregory the Great, in Book Two of his *Dialogues,* depicts the life of St. Benedict of Nursia, who founded the great monastery of Monte Cassino around A.D. 529. This influential hagiographical work gives us a picture of the range of expectations that medieval people had of a saint.

Gregory I, describing the amazing abilities of St. Benedict, remarks almost casually, "Of course he knew God's secrets since he followed God's teaching: For it is written, 'But he who is united to the Lord becomes one spirit with him.' . . . Holy men are not ignorant of God's thought insofar as they are one with God."[20] Because of his humanness, on the one hand, and his access to the very thoughts of God, on the other hand, the saint is in a position to bring together divine power and human need. The saint, because of his immediate access to God, can make predictions, including, in the best classical tradition, that of his own death. He can also heal, bring dead persons to life; he can control demons, even permitting them to reinhabit the person from whom they have been expelled if the conditions the saint prescribes are not met. The saint has intuitive knowledge of material things; he can identify poisoned wine, for example. He can perform astral projections like a shaman. These abilities are explained "reasonably" by Gregory as due to a fact of experience that is "quite clear," namely, that "spirit is more mobile in nature than body," so that Benedict, for the sake of economy, appeared in spirit form to monks whom he wanted to instruct spiritually. The saint can release the souls of the damned, and he can change the weather, not by knowledge or by magic, but, Gregory says, by love. Finally, Gregory makes the curious statement that these miracles can sometimes be performed by saints through their own personal power: "Those who grow close to Almighty God by serving him can sometimes perform miracles through their own power."

The saint accumulates and "stores" power by a combination of ascetic practices and by an "expanded consciousness" that is the result of his participation in the power of God:

> For a soul that beholds the Creator, all creation is narrow in compass. For when a person views the Creator's light, no matter how little of it, all creation becomes small in his eyes. By the light of the inmost vision, the inner recesses of his mind are opened up and so expanded in God that they are above the universe. In fact, the soul of the beholder rises even above itself. When it is caught up above itself in God's light, it is made

ampler within. As it looks down from its height it grasps the smallness of
what it could not take in its lowly state. Therefore, as Benedict gazed at
the fiery globe, he saw angels too returning to heaven. . . . To say that
the world was gathered together before his eyes does not mean that
heaven and earth shrank, but that the mind of the beholder was expanded
so that he could easily see everything below God since he himself was
caught up in God.[21]

But saints do not exercise power only during their lives; they are even
more powerful after their death through their relics, the highly valued
relics of their bodies which contain and communicate power.[22] We have
seen that the earliest Christian martyrdom accounts describe Christians
as gathering and treasuring the corpses or bones of martyrs. By the
middle of the fourth century the practice of hoarding these relics and
treating them as precious objects was noted by pagans as very peculiarly
Christian. The emperor Julian wrote:

> You keep adding many corpses newly dead to the corpses of long ago. You
> have filled the whole world with tombs and sepulchres, . . . the carrying
> of the corpses of the dead through a great assembly of people, in the midst
> of dense crowds, straining the eyesight of all with ill-omened sights of the
> dead. What day so touched by death could be lucky? How, after being
> present at such ceremonies, could anyone approach the gods?[23]

In Gregory's picture of the complete saint, we see again a curious
reworking of the hierarchical view. The saint's power to perform
miracles by his presence, his word, or his touch is achieved by his soul's
cultivated ability to remove itself from the body. Yet the *point* of the
power, as well as its location, is the ability to rectify aspects of the
material, physical world of bodies, places, and objects. Contemplation is
no longer the self-validating supreme activity of human beings but must
result in perceptible benefit to persons and society. Gregory makes
explicit the association of the act of the incarnation of Christ with the
new permeability of the sensible world:

> To bestow such power on earthly human beings, the Creator of heaven
> and earth descended from heaven to earth: and that flesh might judge of
> spiritual things, God, who for humankind's sake was made flesh,
> guaranteed to bestow upon him; for from thence our weakness did rise up
> above itself, when the strength of God was weakened under itself.[24]

The thesis that it was the medieval interpretation of the meaning of
the incarnation that focused the attention of medieval people on the
altered status of the material world and the human body is further

illustrated in the work of the monk, Bede, who as a young child was donated to the monastery of St. Peter at Wearmouth, Great Britain. In his *History of the English Church and People*, Bede undertook to describe the evangelization of the British Isles by Augustine of Canterbury under the careful direction of Gregory the Great. Bede's account underlines the way in which the Christianization of the British Isles progressed by a skillful weaving of *sanctus* and *virtus* in the missionary monks. It is simplistic to attribute Bede's miracle accounts merely to the superstitiousness of the author and those he describes. Credulity was a very hard won attitude in Bede's contemporaries. The skepticism of the British tribes and the dramatic evidence that overcame such skepticism is one of the themes of Bede's work.

The monks who undertook to evangelize Britain in the seventh century understood their task to be the conversion of people who understood and valued power. These monks were convinced of the identity of the incarnation of Christ and the effects of the incarnation in the sensible world. The natural world, no longer the habitat of spirits and demons, but now irreversibly the arena of the infinitely greater power demonstrated by the incarnation, was the appropriate medium for the demonstration of the superiority of the Christian faith.

But it was not only the obvious miracles that compelled belief. For Bede, miracles had to occur in the context of a respected life and attractive beliefs. The missionaries headed by Augustine

> were constantly at prayer; they fasted and kept vigils; they preached the word of life to whomsoever they could. They regarded worldly things as of little importance, and [most impressive of all], they accepted only necessary food from those they taught. They practiced what they preached, and were willing to endure any hardship, and even to die for the faith which they proclaimed. A number of heathen, admiring the simplicity of their holy lives and the comfort of their heavenly message, believed and were baptised.[25]

One gets a sense of the specific quality of saintliness as Bede describes the tactics used by Augustine: a combination of teaching, of demonstrating the validity of the faith by holy lives, and of flamboyant miracles which include the winning of battles and the healing of retarded children. As with the two Gregorys, these miracles range from the personal intervention of saintly people to the genuine "materialism" of holy objects and places:

Oswald's great devotion and faith in God was made evident by the miracles that took place after his death. For at the place where he was killed . . . sick men and beasts are healed to this day. Many people took away earth from the place where his body fell, and put it in water, from which sick folk who drank it received great benefit. This practice became so popular that as the earth was gradually removed, a pit was left in which a man could stand. But it is not to be wondered at that the sick received healing at the place of his death, for during his lifetime he never failed to provide for the sick and the needy. . . . Many miracles were reported as having occurred at this spot, or by means of the earth taken from it.[26]

The material world is thus seen to be the valued and appropriate agent of the activity of God's power. Specifically, Bede's view of the human body is defined in his report that Gregory the Great nipped in the bud the heresy of Eutyches, bishop of Constantinople, who taught that in the resurrection our bodies will then be "impalpable, more intangible than wind and air." This spiritualization of the resurrection body was profoundly antagonistic to both Gregory and Bede. Bede reports with satisfaction:

When Gregory heard this, he quoted the example of our Lord's resurrection, and showed logically how this opinion was utterly opposed to the orthodox belief. For the Catholic belief is that the body is transfigured in the glory of immortality and refined by the operation of spiritual power, but remains palpable by reason of its nature.[27]

Not only is the natural world in general the medium and evidence of the operation of God's power in the sensible world, but the human body itself, when the utterly incredible gift of continence has been matched by spiritual acumen, becomes the place of immediate sensible evidence of the already transformed body of the resurrection. The case of Queen Etheldreda is an example. Etheldreda was married to King Egfrid, but "though she lived with him for twelve years, she preserved the glory of perpetual virginity." It is not immediately apparent whether King Egfrid or Queen Etheldreda should be more congratulated for this prodigious feat. In any case, Bede reports that Etheldreda eventually died and was buried, but, not allowed to rest in peace, was exhumed after seventeen years for removal to a newly built church:

When the tomb of the holy and virginal spouse of Christ was opened and her body brought to light, it was found as free from decay as if she had died and been buried that very day. . . . Proof is given by the physician Cynefrid, who was present both at her death and exhumation, and who stated that during her last illness she had a large tumor under her jaw removed. [When the bones were being removed and washed, the physician was called.] There I saw the body of the holy virgin taken from its grave and laid on a bed as though asleep, and when they had uncovered her face, they showed me that the incision . . . had healed. . . . In place of the large gaping wound with which she was buried, there remained only the faint mark of a scar. All the linen cloths in which the body had been wrapped appeared as fresh and new as on the day when they had been placed around her pure body.[28]

The reward may not seem to us commensurate with the sacrifice, but to medieval people the fascination with those who were able to "offer up" the body's most intimate and pleasurable activity was intense. We need not regard this as a devaluation of sexuality. The sacrifice of sex may well be the result of valuing it very highly. If the sacrifice is precisely that of the most highly valued function of human beings, then we can find this metaphysical insistence on the reality of the body in the resurrection, and the prefiguring of the "perfect health of body" in the virginal body of Etheldreda, compatible in every way. The bodies of saints have already become participants in the resurrection, and this fact was immediately available to the senses in very concrete proof!

The society Bede describes is one in which corruption, treachery, and force combined to determine the fate of individuals and of tribes. It was a society in which the most important thing to know about life was its fragility:

When we compare the present life of man with that time of which we have no knowledge, it seems to me like the swift flight of a lone sparrow through the banqueting-hall where you sit in the winter months to dine with your thanes and counselors. Inside there is a comforting fire to warm the room; outside the wintry storms of snow and rain are raging. This sparrow flies swiftly in through one door of the hall, and out through another. While he is inside he is safe from the winter storms; but after a few moments of comfort he vanishes from sight into the darkness whence he came. Similarly, man appears on earth for a little while, but we know nothing of what went before this life, and what follows.[29]

Bede's poignant sense of the fleeting swiftness of life and the importance of making the right choices "on the run" focuses his interest on the human body. In Bede, as in the Gregorys, the natural world and the body constitute the condition in which God's power can be seen to operate. Death, for Bede, "wonderfully concentrated the mind." It has been said that everyone has an idea of what will happen at death, and that this idea, conscious or unconscious, informs everything one does in life. Bede held this view. A letter of Bede's pupil, Cuthbert, later abbot of Wearmouth and Jarrow, describes him as often quoting Scripture texts that reminded one of death, and "he used to arouse our souls by the consideration of our last hour." He also recited to the monks, in their native tongue, the following verse:

> Ere a man go hence
> Faring as all must fare
> None is there more wise,
> More than he ought to be,
> In well considering
> What to his spirit of good or evil
> After his day of death
> Doomed may be.[30]

Deathbed scenes are related with attention to the characteristics of the person, whose soul is revealed before death in insights concerning the world to come and after death by the miracles that validate his or her holiness.

In the early medieval period of Western Christian thought, the body and the natural world assume a new importance. The interest in saints, miracles, and relics of Western early medieval people should be seen in the context of the practical creativity of medieval culture. This interest should also be seen as a continuation and reworking of the late classical description of the status and meaning of the incarnation of Christ. Medieval people saw the altered and enhanced status of the material and sensible world as the result of the participation of God himself in the conditions of space and time. What we have identified as the incarnational view thus recognized and affirmed a dramatic irruption of divinity into the sensible world, a shortcut of the graded stages of ascent to experience of God through contemplation which the classical anthropology and cosmology of the earlier Christian writers had described. Although medieval authors still assume a hierarchical view,[31] their excitement is focused on the concrete effect of the incarnation on the world of sensible experience.

II

Throughout a Christian tradition unbroken to our own time, the Eastern Orthodox Church has not suffered the same problems of rivalry between church and state that have marked so much of Western Christian history. The subordination of ecclesiastical affairs to monarchical control has created an environment different both culturally and religiously for Eastern Christians. We cannot here develop the cultural and social setting of Eastern Orthodoxy in any further detail than to indicate the significance for the thought of the Eastern church of this harmonious coexistence of the sacred and the secular realms, this *synphonia*, as Byzantine authors have characterized it. The fragmentation of politics and culture in the West among agrarian groups had no counterpart in the Byzantine Empire. A central organization dealt more or less effectively with the problems, internal and external, that constantly threatened to disrupt Byzantine society.

In order to understand the anthropology of the Eastern Orthodox Church, and its views of the human body, we will begin with its idea of how to do theology.

The first assumption required of Eastern Orthodox theology is that there is "one changeless truth," its changelessness guaranteed by the changelessness of God. The patristic authors who first drew out the implications of Scripture and the church councils that defined all later Christian doctrine and practice have a far more than abstract authority. Only by accepting the insights of the fathers, in their original wording, can the Orthodox Christian come to understand truth. The fathers, in this sense, are seen as ever-contemporary. In entering the spirit of the fathers through their language, one shares their vision. Although this assumption of the timelessness of truth has often been criticized by Western authors, in practice it is not a mindless swallowing of authority but the creative appropriation of its insights. Also Eastern authors are not unaware that the fathers did not agree on every aspect of Christian faith. Only in areas of agreement among the fathers are their views normative for belief and practice.

A second element of theology in the Eastern church is the identification of theology with contemplation or mysticism. The Western definition in our own day, i.e., that theology is concerned with thinking and religion is concerned with praying, is rejected in the East. Only three men of the Eastern church have been recognized as theologians: John, the disciple of Christ, Gregory Nazianzen, the poet of theology, and Simeon the New Theologian (who died in 1022), "the singer of union with God." These theologians exemplify the insistence that "mysticism and theology sustain and complete each other; either is unthinkable without the other."[32] Scholastic theology in the West in the eleventh century solidified the opinion among Easterners that the undisciplined use of reason betrayed and distorted theological thinking. Simeon wrote:

> You use evasive arguments; you flourish syllogisms; and I will show you that you alter the meaning of holy Scripture and the Fathers by false interpretation, that you follow, not the Fathers, but the heathen. If I wanted to I could bring forward better syllogisms than yours against your scholastical reasonings—but I do not want to. I ask for proofs from the Fathers and what they wrote; you reply with Aristotle and Plato, or even your new doctors. Against them I set up the fishermen with their straightforward utterances, their true wisdom and their apparent foolishness. I will disclose that mystery of godliness that St. Paul looked on as such strong evidence. I will make foolishness of your wisdom with the words, "Leave these vain matters alone. If anyone proclaims a gospel to you other than the gospel you have received, let him be accursed." Thus will you be brought to confusion, and I shall glory in the glory of my fathers, for the Cross has not lost its power, even though the preaching of it seems foolishness to some.[33]

This brings us to a third characteristic of Eastern theology. The Eastern understanding of what constitutes knowledge differs from Western understandings. It is difficult to characterize both in relation to one another without caricaturing either, but it must be attempted. In the West knowledge has been valued as definition, analysis, and as an intellectual excitement with no parallel in the East. This is a difference in emphasis more than in content, because many Western authors have spoken explicitly about the necessity to integrate knowledge, doctrine, and liturgy in the same sense that Eastern authors have done. But in the East, contemplation, liturgical practice, and piety are more closely and constantly woven into the definition of what knowledge is. In addition, Orthodox thought explicitly acknowledges that all our knowledge of God occurs within limits. In the great mystical thinker of the early sixth century, Pseudo-Dionysius the Areopagite, for example, knowledge has the curious task of "affirming the unknowability of what it knows; not in the sense of being unintelligible, but in transcending all understanding."[34]

Two kinds of theological knowledge are described by Eastern Orthodox writers, the *cataphatic*, or way of positive affirmation, and the *apophatic*, the way of negation, which asserts the necessarily metaphorical nature of our knowledge of God. The experiential component of apophatic theology was described by Gregory of Nyssa thus:

It is like a perpendicular cliff of smooth rock, rearing up from the limitless expanse of sea to its top that overhangs the sheer abyss. Imagine what a man feels when he stands right on the edge, and sees that there is no hold for hand or foot: the mind feels in just the same way when, in its quest for the Nature that is outside time and space, it finds that all footholds have been left behind. There is nothing to "take hold of," neither place, nor time, nor dimension, nor anything else, nothing on which thought can take its stand. At every turn the mind feels the ungraspable escape its grasp, it becomes giddy, there is no way out.[35]

Intellectually, apophatic theology recognizes that there are two limiting problems in theology. The first is the problem of language. John of Damascus, in *The Orthodox Faith,* wrote:

> Now one who would speak or hear about God should know beyond any doubt that in what concerns theology . . . not all things are expressible and not all are capable of expression; . . . neither are all things unknowable, nor are they all knowable.[36]

John, therefore, shapes his account of Christian faith by beginning and ending with confessions of what is unknown. On the problem of language he says: "That which can be known is one thing, whereas that which can be said is another, just as it is one thing to speak and another to know." The second problem of theology is thus that what is "known" is not simply what can be articulated, but what can also be appropriated. This problem has two dimensions. First, only what is necessary to salvation can be accurately called "knowledge":

> Since, therefore, God knows all things and provides for each according to his needs, he has revealed to us what was expedient for us to know, whereas that which we were unable to bear, he has withheld. With these things let us be content and in them let us abide and let us not step over the ancient bounds or pass beyond the divine tradition.[37]

Knowledge rightly so called, then, must be the humble appropriation of "what it is expedient for us to know," and not any abstract or theoretical knowledge, whether related to facts or to ideas. Second, the head is not the sole assimilator of knowledge in human beings. Rather, knowledge is to a great extent organic, the understanding that has been worked into the fiber of one's life. Simeon the New Theologian wrote:

> Do not try to describe ineffable matters by words alone, for this is an impossibility, . . . but let us contemplate such matters by activity, labor, and fatigue. . . . In this way we shall be taught the meaning of such things as the sacred mysteries.[38]

This insistence on knowledge as part of the body itself in "activity, labor, and fatigue" is essential to the characteristic Eastern Orthodox view of the body. Knowledge must be salvific personal knowledge, and it must be integrated in the whole person and not only in the intellect.

Balancing this emphasis on "living" theological knowledge is the objectivity of the ecumenical councils, the writings of the fathers, and Holy Scripture. This objectivity is the corrective of personal knowledge which, if only the experiential and contemplative aspect were stressed, could become idiosyncratic and divisive. The theological enterprise is firmly balanced between the exact language of the tradition of the Christian church and the personal appropriation of this tradition. Heresy is synonymous with "innovation." Maximus the Confessor, the greatest thinker of the seventh century, said, "Every formula and term that is not found in the Fathers is shown to be obviously an innovation."[39] The semantic truth that different language refers to different things is an important one.

We will now turn from these assumptions to the views of the human body for which they form the context. And we must, I think, begin by describing the Christology that is fundamental to it. Trying to characterize without caricaturing, we should say that Eastern Christology is not essentially different from Western but is interpreted differently. "He became what we are in order that we might become what he is." This statement represents a common emphasis in both Eastern Orthodoxy and the West.

For the Eastern church, Christology is the basis of anthropology because it is only by understanding the person and work of Christ and the relation of these to humanity that one can understand humanity accurately. In the West, the method has been different. Since Augustine, the method has been to begin with and try to understand humanity, and on this basis then to understand Christ. This difference in starting points has far-reaching repercussions. Both provide important and valuable insights.

Eastern Orthodox Christology begins by affirming that human beings are created in the image of God and that Christ is the visible embodied description of God. Thus it is only from Christ that one can learn the most intimate and important fact of human being, its quality of image. We only learn what it is we image by bringing all our capacities for intellectual and experiential understanding to considering the person and work of Christ. The most central insight we get from contemplating Christ is that "he became what we are in order that we might become

what he is." Because human beings share a common nature with Christ,
a connection that can be realized only in the activity of contemplation,
human being is deified by participation in Christ's divinity. "Ye are
gods." This oft-quoted verse, together with the promise that believers
become "partakers in the divine nature," is the Scriptural basis for the
Eastern affirmation of deification. Now it is important to notice that
deification does not imply cognitive "knowledge" of the being of God,
but participation in the life, or energy, of God. Deification is certainly a
gift of grace, but there is an irreducible human activity involved in the
appropriation of this gift. Maximus the Confessor wrote: "For the Spirit
does not generate a will that is not willing, but transforms into
deification a will that has the desire."[40] Salvation is deification, a
restoration of the image of God that is possible because of the complete
bonding of human and divine in Christ.

Here we must pause to remind ourselves of the two views of human
being and the cosmos examined in the last chapter. We described the
hierarchical view only to set it apart from the incarnational view which
predominated in the early medieval period in the West. We will now
reverse this procedure and characterize the incarnational view in order
to distinguish it from the hierarchical view assumed by Eastern
Orthodoxy. In the incarnational view, there is an implicit hierarchy
which extends from God through angelic beings and human beings to
the material world and to matter itself, which, though still God's
creation, has not yet received life and thus is of lowest value. But the
incarnation of Christ radically collapsed this hierarchy when God
abruptly entered time and space, the world of body and of sense. This
event has altered the material world so that the activity of God within it
is evident to the senses and becomes the center of interest. This
incarnational view does not exclude hierarchical assumptions, but
neither does it focus on either a hierarchy of human being or a cosmic
hierarchy. We did not find in Gregory of Tours, Gregory the Great, or
Bede descriptions of a graded ascent through contemplation to
experience of God. Yet John Climacus in the Eastern church, abbot of
Sinai at the end of the sixth century, composed a treatise for monks in
which he characterized their life as the ascent of a thirty-runged ladder.
Frontispieces of monastic books from this period and later commonly
emphasize a graded ascent to God through virtue and contemplation by
portraying monks climbing and/or falling from a ladder.[41]

The hierarchical emphasis of the Eastern church also focuses very
strongly on the incarnation of Christ and the difference the incarnation

has made in the world of the senses. Yet the emphasis is on participation in the divinity of Christ through *contemplation,* which gathers and directs physical energy as well as the mind's attention. The body and the natural world are included in the mind's experience of God, but there is no sense of the startling irruption of divine power which may bypass the mind's activity, as in our early medieval Western sources. Easterners were not less interested in saints and miracles than Westerners in the medieval period, but they emphasized the contemplative prowess of the Eastern saint where the West stressed ascetic living. One significant indication of this difference can be seen in the later medieval validations of sainthood. In the West the stigmata provided the visible seal of holiness, while in the East transfiguration was the supreme validation of a saint. What a contemporary Easterner has called the "cult of the humanity of Christ"[42] never inspired Eastern saints to the physical imitation of Christ: "No saint of the Eastern Church has ever borne the stigmata."[43] Miracles occurred through the agency of saints, relics, or icons because of the enormous spiritual energy in them. The Eastern insistence on *synergy,* or willing cooperation with the grace of God, features in this as well. If grace is absolutely gratuitous, a view that was never *in practice* the Western view but was nonetheless apparently Augustine's theological position, then the development of concentration in contemplation is not the *sine qua non* of spiritual power as it was in the East.

A further difference of theological models underscores the disagreement of East and West. In the West, Augustine had changed the theological working metaphor from that of a cosmic vision of intimately connected and permeable but *simultaneously* available dynamic levels of reality to the temporal anthropological model of pilgrimage. In the West after Augustine's time, the spatial-hierarchical model was subordinated to the temporal model. Human beings were no longer strangers and pilgrims because of their distance within the hierarchy of being from the Source of being, but they are strangers and pilgrims because of their distance in time from the moment of human fulfillment and beatitude.

The implications of the hierarchical approach for a definition of humankind can be followed in Gregory of Nyssa's *De opificio hominis—The Making of Humankind.* This interesting treatise describes a strongly connected, spatially modeled hierarchy of human being and the cosmos. Gregory begins by showing that the structure of the human body itself testifies to the predominance of reason. Its upright form clearly indicates by the position of the head that reason is the "topmost" quality of the human being. The capacity of the hands to procure food, thus freeing the mouth for speech, also shows a human hierarchy imaged by the body. The passage is worth quoting in full because it gives such a complete picture of each aspect of the hierarchy as well as the way in which lower levels image the higher:

> And here, I think, there is a view of the matter more close to nature, by which we may learn something of the more refined doctrines. For since the most beautiful and supreme good of all is the Divinity itself, to which incline all things which have a tendency towards what is beautiful and good, we therefore say that the mind, as being in the image of the most beautiful, itself also remains in goodness and beauty as long as it partakes as far as is possible in its likeness to the archetype; but if it were at all to depart from this it is deprived of that beauty in which it was. And as we said that the mind was adorned by the likeness of the archetypal beauty, being formed as though it were a mirror to receive the figure of that which it expresses, we consider that the nature which is governed by it [i.e., the body] is attached to the mind in the same relation, and that it too is adorned by the beauty that the mind gives, being, so to say, a mirror of the mirror; and that by it is swayed and sustained the material element of that existence in which the nature is contemplated. Thus so long as one keeps in touch with the other, the communication of the true beauty extends proportionally through the whole series, beautifying by the superior nature that which comes next to it; but when there is any interruption of this beneficent connection, or when, on the contrary, the superior comes to follow the inferior, then is displayed the misshapen character of matter, when it is isolated from nature (for in itself matter is a thing without form or structure), and by its shapelessness is also destroyed that beauty of nature with which it is adorned through the mind; and so the transmission of the ugliness of matter reaches through the nature to the mind itself, so that the image of God is no longer seen in the figure expressed by that which was moulded according to it; for the mind, setting the idea of good like a mirror behind the back, turns off the incident rays of the effulgence of the good, and it receives into itself the impress of the shapelessness of matter.[44]

The image of God, the most intimate and telling fact of human nature, resides most directly in the mind but includes the body as its accurate reflection:

> When the whole person is in a manner conmingled with the love of God, then even his outward appearance in the body, as in a kind of mirror, shows the splendour of his soul.[45]

The hierarchical connection of mind and body makes it possible to say that the entire human being is made in the image of God. Moreover, the image of God is common to all humankind and is the basis of the natural unity of human beings:

> The entire plenitude of humanity was included by the God of all . . . as it were in one body, and this is what the text teaches us which says, "God created humanity, in the image of God created he them"[46]

The original creation of humankind was "as it were in one body," and it is this creation which is rightly said to be in God's image. However, the division into sexes which "God devised for His image" has "no reference to the Divine archetype," but symbolizes the fallen state with all its difficulty of communication. There is no suggestion in Gregory of Nyssa's treatise that one sex is prior to or cosmically higher than the other. Nor is the division into sexes cited as a punishment, but only as God's foreknowledge that human sin would necessitate death and that death would make necessary a "contrivance for increase."[47] Gregory does add, though, that this mode of generation, unfortunately not that of the angels, was the result of human "inclination to material things," an "animal and irrational mode."[48] Not to participate in sexuality, then, is to raise one's human status to the "angelic state," to put it at a distance from "the beasts." Gregory, acknowledging that he does not participate in the "angelic life," envies those who do.

His treatise *On Virginity* makes this association of death and sex even more explicit. His opening argument concerns the inevitable distraction of worldly cares that are the result of marriage. But his argument progresses to the observation that

> in the cases where it is possible at once to be true to the diviner love, and to embrace wedlock, there is no reason for setting aside this dispensation of nature and misrepresenting as abominable that which is honorable.[49]

The logical result of this argument is that only those who cannot manage to put first things first should contemplate giving up marriage for a life of continence: "It would be well, then, for the weaker brethren to fly to virginity as to an impregnable fortress, rather than to descend into the career of life's consequences and invite temptations to do their worst upon them."[50] But this argument is not Gregory's main presentation of the benefits of continence. Those who lead the continent life, he says, by not participating in sex, do not participate in death. Again, a rather long quotation seems well worth our while.

We should wean ourselves from this life in the flesh, which has an inevitable follower, death; and we should search for a manner of life that does not bring death in its train. Now the life of virginity is such a life. For those who are joined to the Spirit, life and immortality are produced instead of children. . . . This *life*, then, which is *stronger than the power of death*, is, to those who think, the preferable one. The physical bringing of children into the world—I speak without wishing to offend—is as much a starting point of death as of life; because from the moment of birth the process of dying commences. But those who, by virginity, have desisted from this process have drawn within themselves the boundary-line of death, and by their own deed have checked his advance; they have made themselves, in fact, a frontier between life and death, and a barrier too, which thwarts him . . . *virginity is stronger than death;* and that body is rightly named undying which does not lend its service to a dying world.

The life of virginity already enjoys

a certain requisite glory of all the blessed results of our resurrection. For the Lord has announced that the life after our resurrection shall be that of the angels. Now the peculiarity of the angelic nature is that they are strangers to marriage.[51]

Although Gregory of Nyssa selects continence as among the most fruitful ascetic practices, so that he can even say the virgin is "exempt" from "avarice, envy, anger, hatred, and everything of the kind," he is not eager for other ascetic practices which would undermine the body's energy and vitality. He advises only temperance, and this as much for the good of the body as for the soul: "The pleasures of eating and drinking, leading to boundless excess, inflict upon the body the doom of the most dreadful sufferings; for overindulgence is the parent of most of the painful diseases."[52] The rule of temperance, Gregory says, should caution us against either the indulgence of appetites or their severe restriction:

We should be equally on our guard against either over-amount, neither stifling the mind beneath the wound of the flesh, nor, on the other hand, by gratuitously inflicting weakenings sapping and lowering the powers, so that it can have no thought but of the body's pain.[53]

But we must be careful to notice that despite Gregory's preference for an "angelic life" of continence which would break the hegemony of sex and death over human beings, his treatment of death in *The Making of Humankind* does not find death a welcome release from the body. The human body, although at death it dissolves "into the elements of the universe,"[54] is "wedded" to the soul, and the soul is "disposed to cling to and long for" it. By a sort of spiritual gravity which Gregory describes as "a certain secret and close relationship and power of recognition," the soul in the resurrection "attracts again to itself that which is its own and properly belongs to it."[55] After some examples from the natural world corroborating and illustrating this process, Gregory remarks that the resurrection is already experiential because in human gestation and birth an enormous change of body has occurred.

Gregory's treatise draws to a close with a criticism of a theory, which we recognize as Origen's, that the fall consisted of "departure from communion with good" into a body; he is also critical of the Genesis account of the body being created before the soul so that the "soul is second to body."[56] Rather, "as human being is one, the being consisting of soul and body, we are to suppose that the beginning of its existence is one, common to both parts."[57] After an extended discussion of the physical construction of bodies, Gregory concludes with an account of the process by which body and soul "grew" together:

> For our purpose was to show that the seminal cause of our constitution is neither a soul without a body nor a body without a soul, but that, from animated and living bodies, it is generated at the first as a living and animate being, and that our humanity takes it and cherishes it like a nursling with the resources she herself possesses, and it thus grows on both sides and makes its growth manifest correspondingly in either part—for it at once displays . . . the power of the soul that is interwoven in it, appearing at first obscurely, but afterwards increasing in radiance concurrently with the perfecting of the work.[58]

Describing the careful chipping of a precious stone by a stone-carver to bring out its full beauty, Gregory likens this long, painstaking process to the gradual perfecting of body and soul that restores the image of God, an image that "would have been perfect from the beginning had our nature not been maimed by evil."

> Thus our community in that generation which is subject to passion and of animal nature, brings it about that the divine image does not at once shine forth at our formation, but brings human beings to perfection by a certain method and sequence, through those attributes of the soul which are material and belong rather to the animal creation.[59]

The trouble with the body, then, for Gregory of Nyssa, is sex—which actualizes humanity's connection to the material world—and death, which obliterates the body's life. But the essence of the body transcends even death. Just at the point where we might expect a spiritualizing interpretation of the resurrection body from Gregory, he espouses what one contemporary author has called an "excessive realism."[60] In *On the Soul and the Resurrection*, Gregory describes the soul as retrieving even the material elements of the body in the resurrection. The very materiality of the body can be carried into the resurrection body.[61] It is sex and death which will not have any part in the resurrection, when in the resurrected body human beings will attain to "the life of the angels."

We have explored Gregory of Nyssa's exposition of human being in some detail because of the usefulness of his treatment of the body for our understanding of the part of the body in the hierarchical view of the cosmos. The spatial imagery of the hierarchical view allows emphasis to be put on the availability of full participation in the highest activity of human beings, i.e., in the vision of God. The possibility that the body, as image of the soul, can be caught up in the soul's energy of delight in God is a present and real one. The life of the resurrection is already enjoyed by those who live the angelic life here. In this hierarchical view there is no circumventing of the orderly ladder of being, but every rung of the ladder is transformed by a person's choice to direct the energy of one's attention and affection to the source of the whole. This view of the body is in marked contrast to Augustine's temporally modeled view of the body as the aspect of human being which makes the person painfully aware that we do not yet share in the happiness of the resurrection.

We should notice, then, that although the insistence of Eastern Orthodox thinkers that contemplation is the one human activity which actualizes our connection to God *seems* to disparage the body as an integral aspect of our being, the result of this focus on contemplation is to include the body in the already-transformed life. A fourteenth-century Orthodox monk and mystic, Gregory Palamas, wrote:

> If the body is to partake with the soul in the ineffable benefits of the world to come, it is certain that it must participate in them as far as possible for now. . . . For the body also has an experience of divine things when the passionate forces of the soul are not put to death but transformed and sanctified.[62]

In "transcending" the body, the Eastern Orthodox Christian is simultaneously aware of the importance of the body in the liturgy, in the mystical experience of prayer, and, in a few saints, in a visible transfiguration in which the body is bathed in light. For example, in the method of hesychasm in the Eastern church prayer becomes a "conscious and constant attitude"—perpetual, "as uninterrupted as breathing or the beating of the heart."[63] But breathing is not used merely as a metaphor for a continuous life-giving process. With the intake of each breath, the hesychastic prayer is intimately integrated with the physical vitality of the body so that it is incorporated into the most primary operation of the body: "O Lord Jesus Christ, Son of God, have mercy on me a sinner." Bodily postures also play an important part in the concentration of attention required in this exercise, which seeks to integrate body and soul, not just conceptually, but very concretely by coordinating the vital energy of the body with the concentrated life of the soul. To my knowledge, no such conscious integration of soul and body has been emphasized in Western contemplative practice.

The hierarchical view of human being and the cosmos encourages a more positive view of the body as capable of integration into the spiritual life of the soul than does the incarnational view that postpones the complete integration of soul and body until the resurrection and maintains either an uncomfortable alliance between them or a collapse of one into the other in the "materialism" of miracles.

Keeping in mind that the interest in saints, miracles, and icons of the medieval Byzantine church has different assumptions and a different view of the results of the incarnation, we will look at one further implication of the Eastern view of the body. We have said that the incarnational view of Western medieval Christendom was essentially an interpretation of the Christological concerns of earlier centuries, a translation into practical terms of the understanding that the human body and the natural world could be expected to act differently, to demonstrate their new status, as the result of God's participation in the material and physical world in the incarnation of Christ.[64] In the East, similar expectations existed and have shaped devotional practice. The iconoclastic controversy of the eighth and ninth centuries gave rise to some important understandings of the incarnation which we will now briefly explore.

We cannot follow here the course of the arguments for and against the icons of Christ, the Virgin, and the saints between iconodules and iconoclasts.[65] Nor can we analyze the political conditions that played such an important role in the outcome of the controversy. What interests us here is the appeal, central to the argument for icons,[66] to the incarnation and its effect on the material world:

> The Christian cannot be an idolator, says John Damascene, for . . . when God is seen clothed in flesh and conversing with men I make an image of

God whom I see. I do not worship matter, I worship the God of matter who became matter for my sake and deigned to inhabit matter, who worked out my salvation through matter.[67]

The claim of the Eastern church that in the incarnation matter has been redeemed and has a new status of cooperation in the life of the spirit is strongly stated in another quotation from John of Damascus:

As we are composed of soul and body and our soul does not stand alone, but is, as it were, shrouded by a veil, it is impossible for us to arrive at intellectual conceptions without corporeal things. Just as we listen with our bodily ears to physical words and understand spiritual things, so *through corporeal vision we come to the spiritual.* On this account Christ took a body and a soul, as man has both one and the other. And baptism is likewise double, of water and the spirit. So is communion and prayer and psalmody; everything has a double signification, a corporeal and a spiritual.[68]

The connection between the incarnation and the veneration of icons in the iconoclastic controversy is best stated by a contemporary Eastern Orthodox writer: "The representation of Christ is of special theological significance, as an affirmation of His Incarnation. To reject Christ's icon is virtually to deny His Incarnation; to accept and venerate it is to affirm and recall His Incarnation."[69]

The theological concern of the iconoclasts can be illustrated by the following story. In the *Institutes* John Cassian relates a touching incident concerning the Anthropomorphite heresy of the Egyptian desert in the early fifth century that illustrates the attachment of an illiterate monk to visual aids. The monk Sarapion, an old man of saintly life, could not be persuaded by his Abba to abandon the use of icons: "To Sarapion the view seemed a novelty, not found in tradition." A visiting scholar was asked to explicate the verse in Genesis: 'Let us make man in our own image and likeness':

Photinus explained how all the leaders of the churches understood the text spiritually, not literally nor crudely, and made a long speech adducing numerous proofs from Scripture. "That unmeasurable, incomprehensible, invisible majesty cannot be limited by a human frame or likeness. His nature is incorporeal, uncompounded, simple, and cannot be seen by human eyes nor conceived adequately by a human mind."

At last old Sarapion was moved by the numerous and convincing assertions of this learned man, and consented to the traditional faith of Catholics. . . . When we stood up to give thanks to the Lord in prayer, the old man felt mentally bewildered at having to pray, because he could no longer sense in his heart the anthropomorphic image of God which he had always before his mind's eye when praying. Suddenly he broke into bitter weeping and sobbing, and throwing himself prostrate on the ground with groans, cried: "Woe is me! They have taken my God away from me, and I have none to grasp and I know not whom to adore or to address."[70]

The temptation of the incarnational view is manifested by old Sarapion. The identification of God with the material object of devotion represents a shortcut not permitted by the hierarchical view. The concern of the iconoclasts was precisely this loss of the hierarchy to material objects. But the iconodules were concerned that the system of images God himself had created and reinforced by the incarnation needed to be restored.[71] An image of Christ that displayed his integration of human and divine being was the appropriate reminder of Christ's work in redemption. Such an image, moreover, has great devotional value:

> Many times, doubtless, when we do not have in mind the passion of our Lord, upon seeing the icon of Christ's crucifixion, we recall His saving suffering and fall down and worship, not the material, but that which is represented—just as we do not venerate the material of the book of the Gospels, nor the matter of the Cross, but that which these represent.[72]

The hierarchical view would be incomplete without the material imaging of spiritual realities. The iconoclasts, who claimed to worship the invisible and spiritual God in a spiritual way, omitted a rung in the ladder of ascent to God. John of Damascus wrote: "Perhaps you are sublime and able to transcend what is material, . . . but I, since I am a human being and bear a body, want to deal with holy things and behold them in a bodily manner."[73]

Throughout our discussion of images we have been suggesting another important reason for the use of icons, the educative function of artistic representation. Although we often hear it argued that only illiterates need "visual aids," we must remember the Orthodox distrust of words alone to express theological insights.[74] Nicephorus wrote that, precisely because they are nonverbal, icons convey "theological knowledge."

> They are expressive of the silence of God, exhibiting in themselves the ineffability of a mystery that transcends being. Without ceasing and without silence they praise the goodness of God, in the venerable and thrice-illumined melody of theology.[75]

While words educate and shape conceptual faculties, images balance this by educating the emotions through the artistic form. The emotions, not the mind alone, are engaged by participation of all the senses in the veneration of icons and relics. In the words of Gregory of Nyssa:

> Those who behold them embrace, as it were, the living body itself in full flower. They bring eye, mouth, ear, all their senses into play. And then, shedding tears of reverence and passion, they address to the martyr their prayer of intercession as though he were alive and present.[76]

John of Damascus, in his argument for the necessity of images, describes that coordination of intellect and emotions which is so vital to Eastern Orthodoxy:

> The image speaks to the sight as words to the ear: it brings us understanding. . . . I have not many books nor time for study and I go into a church, the common refuge of souls, my mind wearied with conflicting thoughts. I see before me a beautiful picture and the sight refreshes me and induces me to glorify God. I marvel at the martyr's endurance, at his reward, and fired with burning zeal I fall down to adore God through his martyr and receive a grace of salvation. . . . The representations of the saints are not our gods, but books which lie open and are venerated in churches in order to remind us of God and lead us to worship Him.[77]

Images, then, have variable value. They are necessary because of "the dullness of our body," and their use is as "books of the illiterate." The hierarchical view assumes, on the other hand, that the material world of objects is fully capable of imaging the spiritual world. The iconoclasts argued that because of the seductive quality of visual icons, the cosmic series of images should be limited to uses well below those of the mind's imaging of God in contemplation. To the iconodules, this eliminates from contemplation precisely the material world that Christ entered and redeemed.

The power of the visual, which Arnheim has called the "primary mode of thought,"[78] was both the strength and the weakness of the iconodule's argument. Because of the *power* of vision the appropriate metaphor to describe the experience of God was indeed that of "vision." But because of the effectiveness of the visual mode in *attaching* the viewer to its object, the sensible world was also threateningly seductive. The iconodule's solution to the threat of attachment to visual objects was to develop an art designed to point to a reality beyond the artistic object itself. Iconic art distorts representation in order to emphasize spiritual qualities. Characteristically, eyes are large, noses thin, and mouths small. The body is elongated and landscapes are abstract, simplified to their essential elements. Perspective and natural light are suppressed and nonnatural colors are used.[79] It is impossible to look at an icon of the virgin, the Virgin of Vladimir, for example, and to see a purely human woman. This method of "anagogic" distortion, directing us beyond a seen to an unseen reality, contrasts markedly with the rigorously representational religious art of the West, where a crucifixion scene will emphasize the tortured body of the human Christ, a Virgin and child will look like the young neighbors of the Flemish artist, and so on. The intent of the iconic artist is to depict what is *really* happening in the iconic subject, the spiritual event or the essence of the saint, Christ, or the Virgin. Eastern Orthodox descriptions of the artistic technique in icons still consider it representational, however, in that it represents the spiritual plane, which primarily defines all aspects of the scene.[80]

To contemplate an icon is to enter a visual organization of the world of the spiritual. This contemplation requires us to lay aside intellectual modes based on verbal, even metaphoric expression, which cannot express either the being of God or human emotion. To contemplate an icon, then, is to correct an imbalance caused by training only the intellect and to rejoice in the reflection of the beauty of God in the world of bodies and objects. On the principle that human beings become *like* what we habitually contemplate,[81] the contemplation of icons trains persons to understand and identify with the spiritual energy that forms the sensible world from within. It also trains persons to understand that the sensible world is always included in the life of the Spirit as its image, just as the human person, made in the image of God, can prepare to be restored to that image by contemplating the Christ, whose life and work make that restoration a present reality.[82]

In A.D. 787, the triumph of the icons, a "triumph of the incarnation," was achieved by the Eastern Orthodox Church in the Seventh Ecumenical Council, held at Nicaea:

> We define with all accuracy and care that the venerable and holy icons be set up like the form of the venerable and life-giving Cross, inasmuch as matter consisting of colors and pebbles and other matter is appropriate in the holy Church of God, on sacred vessels and vestments, walls and panels, in houses and on the roads, as well as the image of our Lord and God and Savior Jesus Christ, of our undefiled Lady the Holy Mother of God, of the angels worthy of honor, and of all the holy and pious men. For the more frequently they are seen by means of pictorial representations

the more those who behold them are aroused to remember and desire their prototypes and to give them greeting and worship of honor—but not the true worship of our faith which befits only the divine nature—but to offer them both incense and candles, in the same way as to the form of the venerable and life-giving Cross and the Holy Gospel books and to the other sacred objects, as was the custom even of the ancients.[83]

Although pastoral concerns and arguments from tradition had fueled both sides in the iconoclastic struggle, it was popular and monastic piety, eventually reinforced by imperial edict, which won the day.

The primacy of contemplation in the Eastern Orthodox Church has focused the attention of Eastern Christians on the eternal present, and has foreshortened the experience of history to paradigmatic events whose essence is available only through the contemplative mode. While Western authors have sought the meaning of God's activity in historic events—in a human saga of suffering and struggle to attain to God that will be complete only eschatologically—the Eastern church has been intent on the transformation of present "reality" through contemplation. In place of the rigorously discursive method of Western thought, the spatial imagery of the Eastern hierarchical view balances visual and verbal concepts so that all the possibilities of being human, even resurrection of the body, are potentially present, if one will but strengthen by contemplation one's connection to the life and energy of God's Spirit.

V

A THIRTEENTH-CENTURY SYNTHESIS

SINCE EARLIEST TIMES, a fruitful tension has existed in Christianity between the experience of new, enhanced life and the organization needed to maintain it. Ignatius of Antioch, with the powerful imagery and breathless pace of one on his way to martyrdom, testified to his experience of the new life in Christ while at the same time his concern for unity in the nascent church led him repetitiously to insist on "one church, one bishop, one Eucharist." The more strongly the new life was felt, the more necessary it was to order it carefully, so that the enthusiasm of Christians did not lead to idiosyncracy and division in teaching and practice. Both the unordered lifefulness of enthusiasts and the sterile orderliness of the Roman civic religions, with which the early Christians were very familiar, were to be avoided.

The new life in Christ and the ordering of this life in the church seemed to early Christians to be results of the incarnation. God's participation in Christ's fully human body and the transformation of Christ's body on earth, after the ascension, into the church—in which Christians participate, in the strong statement of Paul, as "living members"—had altered the cosmic status of human beings. In the fourth and fifth centuries, Christians struggled to describe the content of the life and order implicit in the incarnation. It is difficult for us fully to empathize with the embarrassment felt by late classical people over the disruption of the cosmic order implied in God's taking human form. Would the incarnation fit into a Platonic hierarchy with Christ "placed" as the first emanation of God, one step removed from being fully God, as Arius and others suggested? The definition of Three-Persons-in-One, in which Father, Son, and Spirit occupy the same cosmic "position" even though one of them generates the others was unintelligible to the philosophical minds of the late classical world. And how could a transcendent God participate in the material and physical world? Surely not, many people said, to the extent of being born in the normal human way, digesting and eliminating food as other human beings do, suffering pain and spiritual distress, and dying. The transcendence of God seemed fatally compromised by a Christ completely human and fully divine. The cosmic hierarchy could only be destroyed by the entrance of God into the material world. Enormous shifts of perception are implicit in the definition of the person and work of Christ that finally emerged. In the Trinitarian and Christological controversies of the fourth and fifth centuries, the full humanity and divinity of Christ became irreducibly necessary to the Christian faith.

Early medieval people took discussions of the incarnation one step further than the metaphysics of the earlier period by asking what the *meaning* of God's participation in the world was. Surely, they reasoned, the incarnation has altered the status of the sensible world so that it no longer can be regarded as a trap and the senses as "snares." Surely we should be able to experience, to see, hear, and touch, God's power when it is localized by saintliness in a certain body, place, or object at a particular time. The characteristic temptation of medieval people, fascinated by the results of the incarnation, was to define the activity of God solely as interrupting the normal course of events through miracles. Medieval credulity, infatuated with the concrete effects of the incarnation, often failed to maintain the respectful attitude toward God's transcendence which the hierarchical view had. In the West, between Boethius, who died in A.D. 524, and Bonaventure, who died in A.D. 1274, only a few voices like John Scotus Erigena in the ninth century, reminded Christians of the primary function of reason in Christian faith.

The early medieval fascination with saints, miracles, relics, and icons often confused the intelligible world with the sensible world. The twelfth century had attempted to distinguish these worlds and correct the confusion by reviving hierarchical models of their structure. M. Chenu described this as "a progressive elaboration of the essential distinction between preternatural events and the supernatural order of grace, the latter of which has nothing do with marvels."[1] In the renewed appreciation of reason that accompanied this hierarchical emphasis, the structure of society began to reflect these reasserted values. What Peter Brown has called a "shift from consensus to authority" in judicial matters gradually abandoned judgment by ordeal in favor of authoritative judgment by kings or feudal lords. This new form may not have been any more just than the trial by ordeal, the essential ambiguity of which permitted the community to interpret the trial according to its own values in achieving consensus. But it also reflected increasing confidence in a social hierarchy that imaged one of cosmic scope.[2]

The most heated philosophical debate of the early twelfth century was over the problem of whether objects in the sensible world are what primarily exist or whether the reality of the more general classes to which the individuals belong is greater than that of those individuals. As stated, this problem of the so-called "universals" was insoluble. No one claimed individuals were their own sources of being, reality, and value. And yet the persons and objects of the sensible world seemed inadequately described by a metaphysics that understood them as anemic reflections of extra-sensible realities. The question of universals was, in twelfth-century philosophical form, that question about the meaning and value of the sensible world which lies at the heart of both incarnational and hierarchical interpretations of it. Does abstraction from individuals increase reality, or are these abstractions merely ways to collect individuals into concepts meaningless without them? Those who held the latter view, like Roscellinus and other "nominalists," thought that since universals are derived from our observation of individuals, the *individuals* are the primary reality. Universals have no content without them. For William of Champeaux and the "realists," individuals derive their reality from the class in which they participate. Humanity, for example, precedes and makes possible individual human being. In spite of Abelard's mediating proposal for a solution, the struggle for an integrated description of the sensible and the intelligible worlds was not resolved and came into the thirteenth century in this sharpened form.

Two Christian thinkers in the thirteenth century brought to a climax the problem of resolving the incarnational and hierarchical views. Francis of Assisi was the last and greatest medieval Christian to understand the world within the incarnational framework. Bonaventure, his disciple, despaired of attaining the immediate experience of God that belonged to Francis as a gift of grace, and undertook to reconstruct and reenact Francis' experience with the help of a method incorporating a graded hierarchy of being.

It would be stretching the term to call Francis of Assisi a theologian, yet his life and teaching constitute as strong a statement of the incarnational view of reality as we have seen. Francis emphasized God's direct and immediate activity in the sensible world and the persons and objects of the sensible world as the most accessible and trustworthy gauge of God's power. The world was, for Francis, that *form* in which God may be known, loved, and served. The sensible world, far from distracting a person from the greater reality of abstractions, was the arena in which the activity of God could be discerned. Francis' goal was not to free himself from the sensible world, but to practice holiness in participation in it. One example of the way in which he combined personal winsomeness with the *virtus* of earlier saints is reported by Brother Ugolino di Monte Santa Maria approximately a century after Francis' death. It allows us to see—if not an actual event in the life of Francis—at least that quality of saintliness for which his successors especially valued him, his intimate understanding and empathy with the natural world.

Francis—so goes the story—while in the town of Gubbio, was told about a fierce wolf who regularly devoured both animals and people, so that the town was virtually paralyzed for fear of him. Placing his hope "in the Lord Jesus Christ who is master of all creatures," Francis went out to meet the wolf, which made as if to attack him, but became docile as soon as Francis made the sign of the cross toward him. After some negotiation, Francis came to an understanding with him in which the wolf agreed by nodding his head that the people of the town would feed the wolf, who would never again kill livestock or people. This was so successful that even the dogs of the town stopped barking when the wolf came to collect his food. Turning the event to spiritual account, Francis preached a sermon to the crowd gathered to witness the docile wolf being led into the town. "And so, dear people, come back to the Lord, and do fitting penance, and as God has freed you from the wolf in this world, so he will free you from the devouring fire of hell in the next world."[3]

There is more to the saintliness of Francis' life, though, than his ability to act as peacemaker between various warring parts of the natural world. He is the first saint reported to have received the stigmata. After a vision on Mt. Alverna, his biographer wrote, Francis "retained a most intense ardor and flame of divine love in his heart . . . and a marvelous imprint and image of the Passion of Christ in his flesh."[4] These wounds, it is recorded, gave him "very great joy in his heart [and] . . . unbearable pain to his flesh and physical senses." This *physical* participation in the suffering of Christ was the apex of the incarnational view, although, of course, the stigmata also show what sort of divine activity was valued by the followers of Francis.

What kind of attitude to the body does the increasing interest in the stigmata of Western Christendom after Francis' time imply? Nothing could more effectively demonstrate participation in the sufferings of Christ, nothing, that is, since martyrdom in the early church. Eastern Orthodox Christians during the same period came to consider transfiguration the supreme validation of saintliness. Both East and West emphasized the body's participation in the spirit's sharing of the life of Christ. In the Western fascination with the stigmata we see medieval people aware of the way physical pain "wonderfully concentrates the mind." This sharpening of consciousness explains the insistence of Francis' followers that ecstasy and pain belong together. From Lady Julian, his English contemporary, to Ignatius Loyola, who lived some two hundred years after Francis, medieval Christians understood this.

Secondly, trained as we are in a post-Freudian age to think that pleasure and pain are psychic opposites, it is hard for us to entertain the idea that pleasure and pain may eliminate each other only in the middle ranges of the psyche. In extreme states, as at an earlier time the *Acta* of the martyrs attested, pain and ecstasy can become indistinct. Francis' stigmata witness to the heightening of pain and pleasure in the intensified consciousness of ecstasy. These wounds simultaneously gave Francis "unbearable pain to his flesh and physical senses," and "very great joy in his heart."

Finally, we must recognize that this harsh use of the body is the logical result of a thoroughgoing incarnational view of the Christian life. If the normative salvific act of Christ was characterized by physical suffering, the *imitatio Christi* must involve willingness to take these sufferings upon oneself in all their physical reality. We see at this point as well the problem of the incarnational view when it is thus rigorously interpreted. Curiously enough, the hierarchical view, which pays less attention to the capacity of the body to participate in the life of Christ, is gentler to the body in practice. In the hierarchical view, the body is an afterthought in the spirit's experience of energy and lifefulness. We will see later whether these views may not need to be balanced with each other.

Francis founded his order, but the "second founder" of the Franciscan order changed its character dramatically. Bonaventure, wishing to duplicate Francis' experience of ecstasy without his severe asceticism, aimed to reconstruct it through a process of cumulative experience and stages of understanding that presupposed a hierarchy of being. Preserving the spirit of Francis also required Bonaventure to reinterpret his injunctions against learning. Francis, who had once shocked a group of friars by tearing the pages out of a New Testament so that all could enjoy it simultaneously, had always regarded scholarly learning as virtually indistinguishable from pride. Bonaventure, however, thought learning indispensable to those who lacked Francis' gift of grace. For Francis' asceticism of manual labor he substituted an asceticism of study and learning. He further constructed a *discursive* "road to God" which, in the spirit of Francis, rejected no part of creation, but gathered all levels in its progress. We will observe in Bonaventure's road that at each stage of ascent the person who has accurately apprehended the previous stages can then "see" or experience the next stage. The "knowledge" that Bonaventure describes is thus a matter of direct experience rather than "abstraction," in the sense in which modern people usually use the word.

For Francis, whose mind was "so absorbed in Christ . . . that his soul was manifest in his flesh," these stages were not necessary. Yet even for those who must painstakingly ascend by "steps or progressive movements" it is necessary to remember that the activities of knowing and feeling must be kept together,

> lest perchance he should believe that it suffices to read without unction, speculate without devotion, examine without exaltation, work without piety, know without love, understand without humility, be zealous without divine grace, see without wisdom divinely inspired.[5]

Bonaventure's method is manifest in his injunction that "we must mount Jacob's ladder before descending it." A careful process in which the "eye" is trained to recognize the interconnectedness of the whole universe begins with "the whole sensible world, . . . by which ladder we may mount up to God."[6] Each rung of the metaphysical ladder is matched by a corresponding human capacity and activity. On the level of the sensible world, the opening of the senses is enough to guarantee appropriate understanding:

> He, therefore, who is not illumined by such great splendour of created things is blind; he who is not awakened by such great clamour is deaf; he who does not praise God because of all these effects is mute; he who does not note the First Principle from such great signs is foolish.[7]

If we "let in" the sensible world, we experience delight, and because of the connectedness of all the objects of delight,[8] the very capacity for delight in human beings leads to its supreme object:

> If, then, delight is the conjunction of the harmonious, and the likeness of God alone is the most highly beautiful, pleasant, and wholesome, and if it is united in truth and in inwardness and in plenitude which employs our entire capacity, *obviously it can be seen* that God alone is our true delight, and that we are led back to seeking it from all other delights.[9]

The intentionality of the sensible world implies a universal hierarchy. At the second rung one moves to contemplation of the image of God in the mind. Considering the human operations of the mind's loving, knowing, and remembering itself, "you will be able to see God in yourselves as in an image." When the mind pauses to consider itself, "it rises through itself as through a mirror to the contemplation of the Blessed Trinity,"[10] which is the pure form of the mind's activity of memory, intelligence, and love. Just as the former stage was not a "passing through" but a "seeing in" sensible objects, so the second stage is the discernment of the image of God *in*—and not through—the mind. Further, this stage gathers in the first stage. It is what Bonaventure calls "the recovery of the senses."

> Therefore the soul which believes in, hopes in, and loves Jesus Christ, . . . recovers spiritual hearing and vision: hearing to receive the lessons of Christ, vision to look upon the splendour of his light. When, however, he yearns with hope to receive the spirited Word, through desire and affection he recovers spiritual olfaction. When he embraces the incarnate Word in charity, as one receiving from him delight and passing into him through ecstatic love, he recovers taste and touch. When these senses are recovered, when he sees his spouse and hears, smells, tastes, and embraces him, he can sing like a bride a Canticle of Canticles. . . . *For it occurs in affective experience* rather than in rational consideration.[11]

The last stage in the order of discovery is the first stage in the order of being, reality, and value. Without the training of the earlier stages, the mind's eye cannot see "Being itself."

> Just as the eye, intent upon the various differences of the colors, does not see the light by which it sees the other things, and if it sees it, does not notice it, so the mind's eye, intent upon particular and universal beings, does not notice Being itself, which is beyond all genera, though that comes first before the mind and through it all other things. . . . Just as the

bat's eye behaves in the light, so the eye of the mind behaves before the most obvious things of nature.[12]

But the stages by which, finally, the eye is accustomed to see the pure light of Being itself are not completed when one is able to discern and contemplate Being itself. Bonaventure said that "we must mount Jacob's ladder before descending it." The last stage, and that which alone "strongly leads the mind's eye into the stupor of wonder,"[13] is the gathering of all the stages of objects and capacities into a unified vision, the descending of Jacob's ladder:

> While, therefore, you consider these things one by one in themselves, you have a reason for contemplating the truth; when you compare them with one another, you have the wherewithal to hover in highest wonder; and therefore, that your mind may ascend in wonder to wonderful contemplation, *these things should be considered all together.*[14]

The process of coming to knowledge is, for Bonaventure, initiated and completed by love. Indeed, in the highest stage, the unifying activity is one in which "all intellectual operations should be abandoned, and the whole height of our affection should be transferred and transformed into God."[15] The assumption Bonaventure needs in order to move from one order of being to another is the hierarchical assumption of the intimate connection of the whole process and the strengthening in each higher stage of being, reality, and value.

It is important to remember that Bonaventure's hierarchy results from his longing to attain discursively to Francis' immediate incarnational experience. The two views of self and world, of Christian faith and the meaning of the incarnation, are not as contradictory as they appeared when we were discussing the earlier medieval period. And yet they produce very different ideas of the meaning and value of the human body. In the incarnational view, the human body is important as the locus of struggle, trial, and the victory of resurrection. In the hierarchical view, the body is less important, but shares in the soul's affection and attention as its perfect reflection. Bonaventure's hierarchical evaluation of the role of the body yields a different result for the person who follows it rather than Francis' experience of ecstasy. For Bonaventure, the power of God by which being is conferred on the sensible world always radiates in an orderly way through a metaphysical "ladder of being," from God, through the ranks of angelic beings, to the rational mind, and from the mind to the body. This ladder is continuous, intimately connected through the gradations of being that comprise it.

There are no blank spaces and no shortcuts. For example, there must be angels, because something must occupy the metaphysical "space" between God, who is pure spirit and uncreated, and humans, who are created combinations of spirit and matter. There must be created, purely spiritual beings on that rung. On the other hand, evil cannot appear anywhere on the hierarchy of being; evil is nonbeing, and as such has no existence. The body, as part of the sensible world, occupies the bottom rung of the ladder. There is permanent ambiguity in this assignment of the human body to the bottom rung: it is the place to start, as Bonaventure described it, but if the sensible world is not seen as the image of intelligible realities, a person will be content to stop on this rung; one will fail to realize one's human potential for the "stupor of wonder" that is the result of contemplating the full hierarchy.

The incarnational view of Francis, on the other hand, constructed the conditions under which the grace of ecstasy could be received by seizing upon the body's energy and vitality and bringing it thus to the point of death. Gilson describes Francis' attitude toward the body:

> Ecstasy is possible only if the soul frees itself for a time from its body, leaving it literally inanimate; and it frees itself only after it has reduced the body to a point of extenuation where it can no longer hold the soul. The life of the ecstatic—and we mean by that a man whose habitual life consists of being in ecstasy as that of the speculative consists in thought—involves, then, such a wearing down of the whole body that the man who leads it could not continue to live without some special grace of the Holy Spirit.[16]

By the thirteenth century, then, two fundamentally different views of the relationship of God and the material world have been clearly articulated. This is the problem that Thomas Aquinas inherited. Thomas changed the earlier medieval question about the way the material/physical world participates in the activity of God to the question of how human beings have access to the various levels of the hierarchy of being. The *Summa Theologiae* is Thomas' summarization and integration of Christian theology. He begins by distinguishing between natural knowledge, which is the product of human reason and philosophical science, and revelation, in which "certain truths which exceed human reason should be made known to human beings." This distinction is not, however, a separation: "Faith presupposes reason as grace presupposes nature."[17] Moreover, there is considerable overlap between natural knowledge and revelation. Revelation makes accessible to faith some truths which, although potentially knowable through reason, "would only be known by a few, and that after a long time, and with the admixture of many errors."[18] In addition, revelation reveals truths not available to human reason—indeed, the most intimate and important truth of all, that human life is directed to God, "as to an end that surpasses the grasp of reason." Salvation "depends upon the knowledge of this truth." By analyzing the activity and the objects of natural knowledge and revealed truth, Thomas undertook a description of the relationship of human beings to God which both acknowledged the value of the material world and maintained a hierarchy of being and value. One of Thomas' translators has remarked: "While the depth of a theology may be measured by the pleasure with which it talks of God, its firmness and consequent durability as a structure will always be measured by its analysis of what man is."[19] Our attention will be on Thomas' analysis of human being.

Thomas distinguished two operations and two objects in the human struggle to understand and act in the world. The rational mind is intrinsically, as Aristotle taught, *ordered to* the objects of its inquiry. Thomas protected the autonomy of reason in its proper sphere of operation,[20] but he limited it to this sphere. The rational mind is the appropriate tool for exploring both the sensible world and its own operation. But mysteries such as the Trinity and the incarnation are inadequately and inappropriately approached by the rational mind. Not susceptible of proof, of comprehension, or even of approximate explanation, the mysteries of revelation are to be approached by faith. Philosophizing and theologizing are thus different in fundamental ways:

> A philosopher and a theologian pursue different interests; one looks for inherently natural characteristics, the other for relations opening out to God. Even when they look at the same thing their point of view is different. The philosopher starts from proximate causes, the theologian from the first cause as divinely revealed; his concern is the manifestation of God's omnipotence and glory. . . . They also follow different courses, for philosophy takes creatures in themselves and thence infers truths about God; creatures come at the start, God at the end. The movement of theology is the reverse; God comes first, the creature afterwards.[21]

What then is the relationship of the operations and objects of reason and faith? How does Thomas avoid dualism and hold together the two operations and objects which he has distinguished? "Our enterprise," he wrote, "should be to draw out the analogies between the discoveries of reason and the commands of faith."[22] "Truths above reason can be believed on authority alone; where that is lacking we have to take hints from the workings of nature."[23] Thomas, like Bonaventure, proposes a system of analogies by which each lower level in the hierarchy of being reflects the higher stages, not with a precision which would permit us to consider analogies as providing "demonstration or complete understanding,"[24] but yet with enough accuracy to sustain faith.

> We know incorporeal realities, which have no sense images, by analogy with sensible bodies, which do have images, just as we understand truth in the abstract by a consideration of things in which we see truth. God we know, according to Dionysius, as cause about which we ascribe the utmost perfection and negate any limit. Furthermore we cannot, in our present state, know other incorporeals except negatively and by analogy with corporeal realities. Thus, when we understand anything of these beings, we necessarily have to turn to images of sensible bodies even though they do not themselves have such images.[25]

Analogies make faith possible, but the ability to know God is a gift of grace, not of the analogies by which reason unaided seeks to understand God. Thomas manages in this way to affirm the value of the world of the senses while yet preserving a hierarchy of being. Analogy is not identity; divine help is not a shortcut on the "road to God," nor does it abbreviate the ladder of being. Rather,

> divine help is the influence of the first cause on secondary causes, and of a principle cause on instrumental causes; in both cases the nature of the subordinate cause is respected.[26]

Thomas' description of the meaning and value of the human body reflects Bonaventure's definition of hierarchy: "A hierarchy is an ordered power of sacred and rational realities, which preserves for those who are subordinate their proper authority" (*Commentary on the Sentences*, 2.9). Just as he was concerned to protect the sphere of human reason by defining and delimiting it, so Thomas protects the place of the human body by "preserving its proper authority."

In the context of his discussion of the operation of reason, by which the sensible world is understood, and faith, by which revelation is accepted, the philosophical treatment of the human body is preliminary to the theological treatment of it as part of the human being. It is important not to confuse these with each other. On the one hand, Thomas explores human being through observation and the interpretation of experience, i.e., from a purely philosophical point of view. On the other hand, he wants, especially in describing the creation of the first human beings, to understand the Scriptural account of human origins. In both his philosophical and his theological accounts, Thomas corrects and integrates an incarnational view, as we have defined it, with a hierarchical view of human being. Philosophically, Thomas corrects Aristotle's empirical description with Plato's metaphysical one. Theologically, Thomas' account of creation, the fall, and redemption as the essential revealed data about human being results from his concern to demonstrate the distinctness and the complementarity of reason and faith, natural knowledge and revelation, and body and soul.

The order of the *Summa Theologiae* is that of the first chapter of Genesis; the treatise on human being occurs in a discussion of the different days of creation. As one of Thomas' modern interpreters has pointed out,

> St. Thomas works with two apparently irreconcilable principles; first, that man is a material and animal substance; second, that his single soul, composing a natural unity with his body, is spiritual. The contrasted themes run throughout his teaching: it was this part of it his contemporaries found most contentious.[27]

The "two apparently irreconcilable principles" with which Thomas worked come, as we will see, from his wish to protect both the hierarchical view and an incarnational understanding of the integrity and value of body. His agenda is simultaneously to distinguish soul from body, but to insist on their natural unity in human beings. Whether or not these are irreconcilable will emerge as we examine his discussion of soul and body.

Thomas shows his continuity with classical philosophy in his anxiety to avoid a "mixture" of body and soul that would confuse functions with objects: "In any real mixture the component parts no longer subsist." The way to describe a unity is not to erase the distinctness of its parts, but to demonstrate the complementary activity of its components. As in classical philosophy, he begins by defining soul and body in relation to each other. He rejects Plato's formula: "the soul is the person" *(animam esse hominem)*. This definition assumes that the soul's prerogative is activity and the body's is passivity, even in sensation. Thomas cannot allow what he considers the activity of the whole human being to be attributed to a part of it. Neither is the description of the soul as "using a body" accurate.[28] The soul is not united to the body as its "motor."[29] Thomas adopts, rather, Aristotle's distinction that the soul is the *form* of the body:

The reason for this is that what a thing actually does depends on what it actually has to give. . . . Now it is obvious that the soul is the prime endowment by virtue of which a body has life. Life manifests its presence through different activities at different levels, but the soul is the ultimate principle by which we conduct every one of life's activities; the soul is the ultimate motive factor behind nutrition, sensation, and movement from place to place, and the same holds true of the act of understanding. So that this prime factor in intellectual activity, whether we call it mind or intellectual soul, is the formative principle of the body.[30]

Because the soul unifies and coordinates the body's activity as well as its own, the soul is that aspect of the human being which orchestrates the whole human operation. The analysis into "soul" and "body" distinguishes two realities, a spiritual and a material, neither of which could subsist without the other under the conditions of human life as we know it. The substance of the human being, then, consists of soul and body together, and in this sense the spiritual and the material aspects have a mutual dependency. The soul's dependency on the body has to do not only with the need of bodily organs by which to perceive the objects of the sensible world[31] but also with the soul's integrity as a part of the human being:

It is not the soul, properly speaking, that belongs to the species, but rather the composite of soul and body.[32]

In addition, the activity of the mind depends on the health of the body: "There is no free play of the mind except when the senses are fit and vigorous."[33]

A further interesting evidence of Thomas' insistence on presenting a picture of human being which fully acknowledges and integrates body and soul and which is congruent with the central fact of Christian faith, the incarnation, is his description of the sense of touch as the human sense that both distinguishes human beings from animals and demonstrates degrees of intelligence among them:

There are animals with better eyesight, hearing, and sense of smell than man, but his sense of touch has greater assurance than theirs. *Because he has the finest touch,* he is the most prudent of the animals. And among men themselves, it is *because of the sense of touch,* rather than the other senses, that some are more ingenious than others. Rough-skinned and coarse-textured people are mentally rather inept, unlike those with a sensitive skin and delicate touch.

Touch is the foundation of all the other senses. A good touch results from a good complexion or temperament. *Excellence of mind follows from bodily complexion,* for every form is proportioned to its matter. People with a good sense of touch are therefore of a higher soul and clearer mind.[34]

In his discussion of the relationship of intellect to touch, a discussion in which "excellence of mind" apparently is determined by, rather than determining of, a "delicate touch," which in turn is the result, not the cause, of a "good complexion," we even find an excess of incarnational thinking. Such assertions about the soul's "biological predisposition" make us distinctly uncomfortable.

It is also clear that, for Thomas, the soul's connection with the body is permanent:

It belongs to the very essence of the soul to be united to a body, just as it belongs to a light body to float upwards. And just as a light body remains light when forcibly displaced, and thus retains its aptitude and tendency for the location proper to it, in the same way the human soul, remaining in its own existence after separation from the body, has a natural aptitude and a natural tendency to embodiment.[35]

There is also a sense in which the soul is *not* dependent on the body. The mind, the intellectual aspect of the soul, "does not operate as a part of a bodily organ," and therefore its dependency on the body, strong as it is, is limited to the requirements for exercise of reason:

Each person experiences in himself that when he attempts to understand a subject he must practice it and use images as examples to hold his attention. The reason is this: the proper objects of the human mind are the meanings existing in his material environment. These exist only in individuals and therefore cannot be known completely and truly except as there embodied. Now the individual is perceived through sense and imagination.[36]

Thus:

Though the soul's intrinsic existence does not depend on the body, this union appears most necessary for the sake of its proper activity, which is to understand.[37]

But "such rational knowledge cannot comprehend our last end. . . . However expert our knowledge about these material objects, there would always remain a desire to know more." Our rational understanding, whose proper object is the comprehension of sensible objects, often recognizes its inadequacy even in this sphere:

Even among sensible objects there are many whose inner constitution we cannot explain with any certainty, about others we have an inkling, but about some we are blankly ignorant. Hence our restlessness and desire for more perfect knowledge. *Yet is it impossible for a natural desire to be pointless.* Our last end can be achieved only if the natural desire of the mind to know is actualized and stilled by an active principle nobler than anything that is part of us or of our sort of world. . . . Our natural desire, therefore, will not be quieted until we know the first cause, not from reflections, but by its very essence. The first cause is God. Therefore, the ultimate end of rational creatures is the vision of the essence of God.[38]

At this point, the incarnational standpoint is corrected with the hierarchical view: "The human soul . . . is not a form immersed in physical matter or wholly swallowed up by it. So nothing prevents it from having some non-bodily activity, even though the soul's essence is to inform a body."[39] Now in its cosmic setting, the human soul is the highest aspect of the forms that govern material creation but lowest in the intellectual order. Thomas corrects and balances the incarnational view by placing it firmly in the context of a cosmic hierarchy. Even his theological method reflects and assumes hierarchical order. As James Collins has pointed out, systematization is a denial of imperfections.[40] The faith that a complete picture of God, the world, and human being can be systematically presented is the faith that one is describing a perfect universe, one in which there are neither gaps nor contradictions. As Thomas said, "The universe would not be perfect if it did not exhibit every grade of being."[41] Also, the cosmic niche occupied by human beings may not be disrupted by higher beings. In his discussion of free will, Thomas claims that God cannot compel human assent. A rigorously hierarchical universe of being protects, as we have seen, the position and capacities of each level of being:

Divine Providence manages all things according to the proper mode of their functioning. Where human beings are concerned, their freedom and responsibility must be safeguarded, and therefore the employment of force is out of the question. Notice that divine help is the influence of the first cause on secondary causes, and of a principal cause on instrumental causes; *in both cases the nature of the subordinate cause is respected.* . . . Providence does not suppress secondary causes, but achieves its effects by subordinating their nature to itself.[42]

The principle of the hierarchical view has been accurately and succinctly stated by Gilson: "The way to keep anything from being lost is to put everything in its place."[43]

Yet the danger of a rigid hierarchical operation in which God is limited to acting through secondary causes is a determinism in which "physical forms . . . can neither be changed nor interrupted in their action by higher influences from outside, and . . . nothing can break the determinism which links them in a chain." Thomas corrects the hierarchical view with the incarnational affirmation: "God operates through secondary causes, but beyond shadow of doubt is quite able to manage without them. He can break the common and customary rhythm of nature by producing natural effects or fresh effects of a different kind."[44]

> From these three premises, that God is the complete cause of natural realities, that he has distinct knowledge of each and all, and that, uncompelled by natural necessity, he works voluntarily, it follows that he can produce particular effects apart from the ordinary run of nature.[45]

And yet the effect of Thomas' discussion of miracles, even though he is careful to show that the First Cause of the universe can temporarily displace the natural workings of physical things, is to give the miraculous a far less important place than in the incarnational view:

> Miracles lessen the merit of faith to the extent that they argue an unwillingness to believe the Scriptures, a hardness of heart that demands signs and wonders. All the same, it is better for people to turn to the faith because of miracles than to remain altogether in their unbelief. Miracles are signs, not to them that believe, but to them that believe not.[46]

In Thomas, the incarnational view is modified; the sensible world is no longer the primary arena of God's activity.[47] "Divine help," then, is not limited to the "miraculous," but its preferred operation is the orderly activity of the hierarchy: "Divine help is the influence of the first cause on secondary causes; in both cases the nature of the subordinate cause is respected."[48]

The primary function of the sensible world in the modified incarnational view of Thomas Aquinas is to provide analogies that can be used by the rational mind in order to image spiritual truths. Yet the method of analogy would be inappropriate without the hierarchical assumption that each lower level of the hierarchy mirrors those higher. Since there can be no contradiction, but only complementarity between philosophy and theology, "our enterprise should be to draw out the analogies between the discoveries of reason and the commands of faith."[49] Theological truth must be approached by faith as given by authority; theological understanding is a gift of grace. The place of philosophy is to support and encourage faith by making explicit what is implicit in nature, by mirroring intelligible truth. Even the grace of God itself can be understood only by an analogy from nature: "Grace is a glow of soul, a real quality like beauty of body."[50]

The major role of the sensible world, then, is not to startle us into belief, but to provide nondramatic and trustworthy data for its support. Human reason operates on the sensible world, drawing analogies which make faith possible. It is only when this has been done that revelation comes to be seen, not as discontinuous, but as beyond the reach of natural knowledge. The sensible world becomes the proper object of human reason, not the medium of arbitrary and mysterious miracles. Data from the senses, far from being an impediment to the mind's knowledge of ideas, gradually constructs them. Thomas criticizes Plato's doctrine of recollection and its corollary that "traffic" with the body represses the innate ideas with which the soul was born:

> Plato's position, that the human mind is filled with all ideas but is hindered from knowing them because of its union with the body, does not appear altogether well founded. . . . It does not seem possible that the soul could fall into oblivion about such universal natural knowledge were it already really possessed: *nobody forgets what he knows naturally.* . . . Moreover the embarrassment is increased if we suppose that the soul is naturally united with the body, for *that a natural activity should be completely choked by its natural condition is most unlikely.* . . . We should therefore conclude that the soul does not know bodily things through innate ideas.[51]

Though ideas are not "natural," or innate, human desires are. Both the desire for human integrity, for keeping body and soul together, and the desire for God are natural desires, the same desire seen from different vantage points:

> Complete contentment there cannot be unless natural desire is wholly fulfilled. Everything craves what belongs to its nature, and therefore desires its parts to be reunited. Since the human soul is united by nature to the body there is within it a natural appetite for that union. The will could find no perfect rest until the soul and body are joined again.[52]

The desire for God is the making explicit of the polymorphous panoply of human desires:

> In the perfect happiness of heaven nothing more will remain to be desired; in the full enjoyment of God human beings will obtain whatever

they have desired in other things. . . . The desire is stilled; the desire not only for God, but also what lies at the heart of all other desires. Therefore the joy of the blessed is perfectly complete, and more than complete, indeed overfull, for there they find more than is enough for desire.[53]

Natural desires and capacities, although they are needs, are not immediately explicit:

The knowledge that God exists is inborn in us in a general and somewhat confused manner. For God is the final beatitude of human being, and a human being desires beatitude naturally and is also naturally aware of what he desires.[54]

For making explicit what has been implicit, theological knowledge is necessary. Revelation begins to inform human beings about the object implicit in all their desire at the point where reasoning founders. Since, according to Thomas, "pleasure follows congenial activity, and therefore the more vehement the pleasure the more natural the activity,"[55] the pleasure of enjoying God is the most natural and therefore the most "vehement" pleasure human beings can experience.

Since the "natural desires" have their final fulfillment in the enjoyment of God, they point inevitably to theological knowledge, that is, to that aspect of human being which can only be grasped through faith. The Scriptural account of Creation, the Fall, redemption, immortality of the soul, and resurrection of the body completes human self-understanding. We will remark briefly on Thomas' exposition of these because of their importance to an accurate understanding of his view of the body.

Body and soul were created simultaneously. This assertion is consonant with Thomas' Aristotelian view that the soul is the form of the body:

Since the soul is united to body as form and as a natural component of human nature, its creation does not precede its union with the body. By creation God constitutes things in the perfection of their nature. *Apart from the body the soul lacks its natural perfection,* and it would be awkward for it to be created in this condition.[56]

But this incarnational understanding is nuanced; body and soul, although held together, are also clearly distinguished. The original justice that integrated soul and body has been lost through the Fall:

If we face the question steadily, take into account that Divine Providence fits out things properly, and assume that spirit was joined to body in order

that spirit might contain and order matter, we can then be reasonably
persuaded that any threat to the mind's control . . . was forestalled by a
special and supernatural benefit, the original justice with which human
nature was endowed at its first creation.[57]

In one sense the death of the body is natural, and in another it is not, but
is the result of the Fall. Death is intrinsic to being human in that it is a
natural result of the materiality of the human body. But it is unnatural in
that original justice would have prevented it had that grace not been
forfeited through sin.[58] Death is natural to the body itself, but unnatural
to the whole human being: "The soul continues to be when separated
from the body by the failure of body we call death. But *the soul should
not suffer this dislocation* (defectus) *at its origin*."[59]

The hierarchy of soul over body is preserved. The soul's immortality,
and its simultaneous creation and natural unity with the body, mean that
it will experience the body's death as a "dislocation at its origin." Since
the body is "tailor-made" to be the locus of the soul, and "nothing
unnatural can be perpetual,"

> the soul will not be without the body for ever. Since the soul is immortal
> the body should be joined to it again. This is to rise again. The immortality
> of the soul, then, would seem to demand the future resurrection of the
> body.[60]

One of the most telling results of a philosophical or theological system
that attempts to describe an integration of the human body is its idea of
sexuality. Consonant with his affirmation of sexuality as a natural human
activity, Thomas is careful to point out that original sin is not transmitted
by sexual lust. Lust is the symptom rather than the vehicle of original
sin. The way original sin can be *observed* far more clearly than in sexual
lust is in its debilitating effect on human beings. The inertia that Thomas
calls "the langour of nature" is an experiential datum for everyone.
Sexuality shares in, rather than transmits, the debilitation caused by
sin.[61] Similarly, procreation by sexual union is not the result of the Fall:

> For everything that is natural to human beings is neither withdrawn from
> nor given to them by sin. Now it is plain that it is natural to human beings
> in their animal life, which we had even before sin . . . to procreate by
> copulation, as it is to other perfect animals. And this is indicated by the
> organs assigned by nature to this function. And therefore it cannot be said
> of these natural organs, any more than of any other organs, that they
> would not have been used before sin.[62]

Further, Thomas disassociates sexuality and death from being identified as features of fallen existence. Procreation would have been necessary in Eden because of the natural perishability of the human body.[63]

Like Augustine, Thomas says that procreation by copulation would have occurred in the Garden of Eden, but that it would not have been "disfigured by extravagance of desire."[64] The assumption of contemporary people that "extravagance of desire" is pleasurable and that it is the source of sexual pleasure is, to Thomas, a serious and fundamental misconstruction of human experience. Sex, Thomas says, would have been unimaginably more pleasurable were it not affected by that weakening of human nature in the Fall which all aspects of the human being share:

> Not that the pleasurable sensation would have been any less intense, as some say, for the pleasure of sense would have been all the greater, given the greater purity of human nature and *greater sensibility of the body*.[65]

The problem with sexuality as we know it is the anxiety with which "the pleasure urge clutches at the pleasure in an immoderate fashion." Before the Fall, when this would not have been the case, "no particular esteem would have attached to continence."[66] Continence, like lust, is the result of the Fall, an adjustment to an "unnatural" human condition.

It is in the context of this discussion of sexual procreation as an intrinsic part of human existence that Thomas discusses the roles and value of the two sexes. The distinction of the sexes, he says, is for purposes of procreation, which is a necessary and natural human function. Thomas finds that woman was appropriately constructed by God from the rib of Adam in order to signify a companionship with man in which she is neither to exercise authority over him nor to be subordinate to him.[67] The first creation "from the body of the man" is not less honorable than man's creation "from the slime of the earth." Yet it is clear that Thomas considers the theological content of the Genesis account to be the subordination of the female sex, with procreation as its *raison d'être*, "because where most work is concerned man can get help more conveniently from another man than from a woman."[68] The philosophical premise that the primary function of a human being is "understanding things" supports Thomas' assertion that woman was created derivatively from man and thus with lesser capacity in this primary function: "the power of rational discernment is by nature stronger in man."[69] The theological result is that Thomas distinguishes the sense in which the image of God "is found equally in both man and woman as regards that point in which the idea of 'image' is principally realized, namely an intelligent nature," and the sense in which "God's image is found in man in a way in which it is not found in woman; for man is the beginning and end of woman, just as God is the beginning and end of all creation."[70]

These misogynous philosophical and theological results are derived from Thomas' hierarchical concerns. His characteristic commitment to both incarnational unity and hierarchical differentiation colors his discussion of male and female. Women and men have the same value in procreation and in possessing an intelligent nature, yet "the power of rational discernment is stronger in men than in women." Thomas found support for this hierarchical interpretation of the sexes in Scripture. A hierarchical description requires that where there is a natural difference there must be also a different level of being.

Although his own age did not object to this, we certainly may. We cannot expect Thomas to have had the same sociological and anthropological assumptions we do, but we can, I think, see his conclusions here as inadequate for our own time. Augustine, his mentor, in the conclusion of his work on the Trinity, composed a prayer which must be that of all those who attempt to interpret historical ideas, whether Scriptural, patristic, or of later Christian thinkers:

> O Lord, the One God, God the Trinity, whatever I have said in these books as coming from you, may they acknowledge who are yours; but if anything as coming from myself, may you and they who are yours forgive me.

Thomas subscribed to neither the "stupor of wonder" of Bonaventure nor the ecstasy of Francis, but to happiness, beatitude, as the appropriate human end. This is a goal that integrates hierarchical orderliness and human incarnation:

> In speaking of perfect happiness, some have said that no bodily conditions are present, indeed they would have the soul entirely disembodied. . . . But this is unseemly: it is natural for the soul to be united to the body, and one perfection would not exclude another. Therefore we conclude that *integral happiness requires a perfect disposition of body*, both antecedently and consequently. Antecedently, because, as Augustine says, if the flesh, corruptible and a weight upon the soul when the mind is turned away from high heaven, is difficult to manage, nevertheless, he concludes, that very flesh, erstwhile a burden, will then be a glory. Consequently, because from the happiness of the soul there

will be an overflow into the body, quickening it to perfection; as Augustine also says, the soul is made so powerful of its nature that from its fullness of happiness the *vigour of deathlessness pours into the lower nature.*[71]

For Thomas neither an ecstasy that neglects or abuses the body nor contemplative elevation can be the ultimate human end. Predictably, he advocates neither harsh asceticism nor bodily neglect. He describes happiness as an integrated pleasure that occupies a range of human experience between "delight" and "the ease of lover with beloved."[72] Happiness is, he insists, an embodied experience, an *incarnated* experience. Yet there is also a sense in which happiness is the result of ordering one's activity hierarchically: "We are bound to affirm that the blessed see God's very being. Happiness is the ultimate achievement of rational nature."[73] Thomas continues:

A thing is finally complete when it attains its original purpose, and without being forced. . . . A thing reaches God by what it is and by what it does. First, by likeness. This is common to every creature, and the rule is that the closer the likeness to God the more the excellence. Second, by activity, . . . by which I mean the rational creature's activity of knowing and loving God.

The human soul comes directly from God, and therefore finds its happiness by returning direct to God. He must be seen for what he is in himself; seen, that is, without medium which acts as a likeness and representation of the thing known, such as a sense-image in the eye or reflection in a mirror; but not without a medium called the light of glory, which strengthens the mind to have this vision.[74]

Finally, Thomas' philosophical account of the "end" of human being reflects his theological account of it, namely, resurrection. Delight and "the ease of lover with beloved" are enhanced and intensified in the experience of the resurrection:

Let us investigate the properties of the risen body. Our starting point is this, that soul is the substantial form of the body and its active moving principle. It gives the body its human substantial reality, and, not only that, it is the principle of the proper characteristics that follow from its union with the body. The stronger the form, the deeper its impression on the material, the firmer its grip, and the abler it is to resist encroachment from without; the greater are light and warmth, so much the more are the dark and the cold kept out. The blessed soul is joined with God and is at the height of its excellence and vigour, and so it confers on the body, divinely restored to it, substantial being at its best. Entirely possessed by the soul, the body will then be fine and spirited. Then also will it be endowed with the noble lightsomeness of beauty; it will be invulnerable, and no outside forces can damage it; it will be lissome and agile, entirely responsive to the soul, like an instrument in the hands of a skilled player. These are then the four conditions of the glorified body: fineness, radiance, impassibility, and agility.[75]

Thomas' integrated philosophical and theological description of humanity yields a corrected view of it which does not collapse the hierarchical view into an incarnational view, as earlier medieval people had done, and which does not maintain a rigid deterministic hierarchy with no place for the miraculous. Human beings, "ordered to God," must experience God not only by delight of the mind, but with the "quickening and perfecting of the bodily senses."[76]

VI

FOUR TYPES
OF CHRISTIAN ASCETICISM

WE HAVE SO FAR distinguished three attitudes about the human body in the history of Christianity: the body as foil for the soul, the body as problem, and the body as human condition. Christian asceticism takes the body as a condition when it makes it the intimate partner of the soul in learning, suffering, and salvation. Yet this is sometimes colored by the "body as problem" approach, which identifies the soul's lack of integrity with the body's desires for nourishment and propagation, and by the "body as foil" exaggeration of the differences between body and soul for the sake of emphasizing the greater value and beauty of the soul. Clearly these are not so strongly differentiated in historic Christian authors as we would like. In ascetical theology, as in metaphysical, they may from time to time be cited as if they were interchangeable.

Ascetic practice consonant with Christian faith requires that the only condition in which human beings can turn to the source of life and being is as unities of body and soul in which the body is always the "spouse,"[1] the soul's intimate companion. Not every historic author who advocated asceticism was equally clear in denying blame or guilt to the body, but it has been less pejoratively treated in the tradition than popular stereotypes assume. Christian asceticism must also presuppose the permanent *connectedness* of body and soul. The soul should not exhaust itself in caring for the body's needs, but it must care *first* for the body and then proceed to orient the entire human being toward the source of life itself. The connectedness of body and soul was acknowledged in frequent reminders that asceticism is not a question of the soul's imposing its agenda on a recalcitrant body by force of will alone. Ambrose, bishop of Milan at the end of the fourth century, wrote that celibacy is not "under mastery," "for that which is beyond nature is from the author of nature. . . . Virginity cannot be commanded, but must be wished for, for things which are beyond us are matters for prayer rather than under mastery."[2] Although asceticism is a "gift of God," the reception of it is not entirely passive. Receiving from God is highly active, yet the Christian's attention must not be directed to the activity but to the giver.

The four authors with whom we will deal in this chapter illustrate the range of practical ways in which historic Christians have developed these attitudes and assumptions. All found ascetic practice enormously helpful toward goals they considered life-enhancing. Cast in the form of four models of thought, these goals are (1) self-understanding, or exploring the outer edges of the psyche, as seen in a theologian of the Egyptian desert; (2) control of the addictive and deadening agenda of sex, power, and possession, as seen in early monastic rules; (3) gathering and focusing of energy, as described by Augustine; and (4) intensification and concentration of consciousness enabling one to convert oneself to freedom for love and work, as described in Ignatius Loyola.

I

Historians have characterized the men and women who "stampeded" to the Egyptian desert in the fourth and fifth centuries as fleeing from social pressures, economic difficulties, a church diluted by minimally Christianized pagans, or disappointing personal situations. All of these motivations may have played a part in the tremendous attraction they felt for the solitary life. Yet none can completely account for the fascination the desert held for rich and poor, women and men alike.

What were they seeking? Palladius describes their motivation thus:

> Together with the holy fathers who took upon themselves the yoke of the solitary life . . . we commemorate also the marvelous women who led their lives in the Divine Spirit and who waxed exceedingly old, and who with a brave mind brought to an end the strife of the labors of spiritual excellence, according to the Divine manifestation and love, *for they wished to lay hold upon their souls,* and to bind upon their heads the crown of impassibility and holiness.[3]

"They wished to lay hold upon their souls." Evagrius Ponticus, the theologian of the desert movement, gives us a detailed account of the method of the Egyptian desert ascetics at the end of the fourth century. This method combines four techniques for the effective purification of souls. This immediate goal then led to the fulfillment of their ultimate goal, participation in the life of the Kingdom of God. They understood self-knowledge as an intimate part of the search for God, and Evagrius makes this connection clear by his use of the soul as divine image. Only when the psyche is fully explored and understood can it become a clear image of the divine.

The first technique Evagrius describes is that of solitude. Solitude was essential in order to locate the specific causes of the deadening of the soul occasioned by social life. The *Apophthegmata* also testify to this requirement:

> There were three close friends, earnest men, who became monks. One of them chose to make peace between men engaged in controversy. . . . The second chose to visit the sick. The third chose to be quiet in solitude. Then the first, struggling with quarreling opponents, found that he could not heal everyone. And, worn out, he came to the second who was ministering to the sick, and found him flagging in spirit, and unable to fulfil his purpose. And the two agreed and went away to see the third who had become a hermit, and told him their troubles. And they asked him to tell them what progress he had made. And he was silent for a little, and poured water into a cup. And he said, "Look at the water." And it was cloudy. And after a little he said again, "Now look, see how clear the water has become." And when they leant over the water, they saw their faces as in a glass. And then he said to them, "So it is with the man who lives among men. He does not see his own sins because of the turmoil. But when he is at rest, especially in the desert, then he sees his sins."[4]

Secondly, the ascetics of the desert relied upon aphoristic advice from a spiritual guide. Their pithy sayings, elicited by the disciple's request, "Speak to me some word, some phrase," are notable for economy of expression. Their purpose was not to inform or convince the disciple, but rather to be something for the disciple to carry away and dwell with until such time as it had brought about a change in the pattern of ideas. These "words," intended to disrupt the disciple's habitual thought patterns, are often startlingly alogical.

But words, no matter how profoundly insightful, were not effective without a third technique. The disciple must also observe closely the "demons" which operated within the structure of the disciples' emotional life in gratuitous invasions into the individual's consciousness. This "watchfulness" completed a highly effective program of self-knowledge. The necessity for comprehensive and rigorous self-knowledge as a goal on the way to the Kingdom of heaven is described by Evagrius Ponticus:

The Spirit would not make progress nor go forth on that happy sojourn with the band of incorporeal beings unless it should correct its interior. This is so because anxiety arising from interior conflicts is calculated to turn it back upon the things that it has left behind.[5]

The difficulty of achieving self-knowledge was not taken lightly by those who described the process. Those who succeeded in some measure won the title "the great athlete."[6] Evagrius' demonology is the self-conscious language of a science of the psyche. If the spiritual athlete is not to be defeated by the undertow of inner psychic conflict, self-observation and interpretation must be the first order of business.

Although Evagrius distinguished between emotions, or passions, and demons—apparently external incentives to the destructive use of psychic energy—this distinction must not be exaggerated. Demons act through thoughts to arouse emotions, and in this activity are not external at all, but very similar to unconscious agenda. Only the most unremitting observation and accurate interpretation will expose these demons. Evagrius wrote:

> We must take care to recognize the different types of demons and take note of the circumstances of their coming. *We shall know these from our thoughts*. . . . We ought to consider which of the demons are less frequent in their assaults, which are the most vexatious, which are the ones which yield the field more readily and which the more resistant. Finally, we should note which are the ones which make sudden raids and snatch off the spirit to blasphemy. Now it is essential to understand these matters so that when the various evil thoughts set their own proper forces to work we are in a position to address effective words against them, that is to say, *those words which effectively characterize the one present*. And we must do this before they drive us out of our own state of mind. In this manner we shall make ready progress, by the grace of God. We shall pack them off chafing with chagrin and marvelling at our perspicacity.[7]

The agility and ability to observe one's own psyche with this rigor are by the "grace of God," but the interpretation of one's observations and the insights gained are also the gift of God:

> If any monk wishes to take the measure of some of the more fierce demons so as to gain experience in his monastic art, then let him keep careful watch over his thoughts. Let him observe their intensity, their periods of decline, and follow them as they rise and fall. *Let him note well the complexity of his thoughts*, their periodicity, the demons which cause them, with the order of their succession and the nature of their associations. *Then let him ask from Christ the explanations* of these data he has observed.[8]

What, then, is the role of the body in the "ready progress" of self-knowledge? If, as Evagrius wrote, "the ascetic life is the spiritual method for cleansing the affective part of the soul,"[9] for clarifying the mirror in which the image of God can be seen, the *means* for this purification must involve the body:

> For those who have attained to purity of heart *by means of the body* and who in some measure have applied themselves to the contemplation of created things know the grace of the Creator in giving them a body.[10]

Ascetic practices manage the demon of "passion," which keeps the soul from the state of "imperturbable calm" required for unceasing prayer.[11] The demon of passion is the direct antithesis of the soul's delight in prayer, the only energy powerful enough to forestall this delight. The ascetic's main weapon against this adversary is that of ascetic practices. The assumption of all such practices is that the discipline learned by the body is also gained by the soul.

After describing the demons and passions that deflect the soul from its purpose, Evagrius offers antidotes for difficulties ranging from the "wandering mind" to "turbid anger." He cautions that "all these practices are to be engaged in according to due measure and at the appropriate times." Any bodily discipline must be carefully designed to address the exact nature of the spiritual distraction and not applied to the body as if to control an enemy.[12] His suggestions are moderate, temporary, and precisely chosen.[13] They do not follow personal predilection or ability that would permit, for example, one monk to "specialize" in fasting and another in night vigils. Ascetic practices are chosen to correct particular obstacles that hinder prayer.

The only suggestions Evagrius makes are reading, vigils, prayer, fasting, solitude, continence, and limiting one's intake of water. Cassian adds nakedness and poverty to this list. The concern of both authors is to acknowledge the usefulness of some form of bodily discipline, but having done that, to speak against any abuse of the body. We may infer from this concern that such abuse was not unknown even among the Egyptian desert ascetics, who did not at all share the severities of the ascetics of Syria, Mesopotamia, and Palestine.[14] Palladius warned:

> Our holy and most ascetic master stated that the monk should always live as if he were to die on the morrow but at the same time that he should treat his body as if he were to live on with it for many years to come.[15]

The one exception to the temporary nature of these correctives for distraction is continence. Continence is to be a permanent feature of the ascetic's life. The passions of the soul are to be managed in a variety of ways, but the passions of the body are treated by continence. In Evagrius' use, continence implies more than rejection of sexual intercourse; it is also an attitude toward legitimate pleasures. Gluttony, for example, as a "passion of the body," is to be mastered by continence: "Continence has the power of *refusing with joy* every pleasure of the palate."[16] Continence is "refusing with joy" those bodily pleasures which the ascetics had experienced—and many of them had indeed experienced them fully—as spiritually debilitating. But "refusing with joy" relates less to what is refused than to what is desired, namely, the "habitual state of imperturbable calm" in which the soul is "snatched to the heights of intelligible reality . . . by the most intense love."

Evagrius was also very well aware that the passions, the emotions and thoughts that threatened to usurp the spiritual energy of the ascetic, were fully as dangerous for the health of the body as for that of the soul:

> The most fierce passion is anger. In fact, it is defined as a boiling and stirring up of wrath against one who has given injury—or is thought to have done so. It constantly irritates the soul and above all at the time of prayer it seizes the mind and flashes the picture of the offensive person before one's eyes. Then there comes a time when it persists longer, and is transformed into indignation, stirs up alarming experiences at night. This is succeeded by a general debility of the body, malnutrition with its attendant pallor, and the illusion of being attacked by poisonous wild beasts.[17]

Even the constant fasting and lack of sleep to which Antony subjected himself during a twenty-year period of solitude in the desert—which his biographer may have exaggerated—should be understood in the context of a remark in *Vita Antonii* 14. After Antony had spent twenty years engaged in these austerities in the inner desert, he emerged.

> Those who saw him wondered at the sight, for he had the same habit of body as before, and was neither fat, like a man without exercise, nor lean from fasting and striving with the demons, but was just the same as they had known him before his retirement. And again, his soul was free from blemish, for it was neither contracted as if by grief, nor relaxed by pleasure, nor possessed by laughter nor dejection.

Antony had not aged during his "austerities." His biographer finds this interesting and important. The ascetic who understands the discipline and the "tools of the trade"[18] will benefit both body and soul by the ascetic practices employed. Cassian relates as a warning the story of an ascetic who, deceived by the devil, fasted for two days "unsuitably," and who effected by this abstinence nothing but "useless fatigue of body, and worse, a fatigue which would harm the spirit."[19] Such misuse of ascetic practices was regarded by the desert masters as instigated by the devil himself who incited the ascetic to fascination with the means instead of the end of his profession:

> Sometimes he tries to cheat us with counterfeits, by suggesting that we ought to undertake some good work. . . . Sometimes he suggests excessive or impossible fasts, too long vigils, too many prayers, unsuitable reading, and so brings us to a bad end.[20]

The claim made by the Egyptian desert ascetics was that bodily practices intimately affect the psyche and can be used as a method for exploring one's characteristically well-defended psychic agenda, for understanding those unconscious but powerful insecurities, anxieties, and angers which strip the psyche of energy and undermine its conscious attempts at joyous and loving being. It is not to be denied that there were many cases of ascetics who, carried away by discovering the usefulness of bodily disciplines, abused their bodies. A powerful and effective tool always carries the danger of misuse by becoming a goal instead of a means. But the danger of abuse did not dissuade the desert *ammas* and *abbas* for whom only these disciplines could illuminate the rationalizations and defenses of the unexamined life. Their positive program was described by Palladius:

> So that . . . thou mayest be able to dispel from thy soul all the slumber of error, which comes into being through irrational desire, and all the doubts of the soul in respect of faith, and sluggishness in respect of the things that are useful, and all loathing and littleness of soul concerning habits of virtue, that is to say, keenness of wrath and perturbation and animal ferocity and empty fear.[21]

II

By the end of the fourth century, the individualism of the desert hermits had largely given way, under criticism, to a communal form of ascetic life. Pachomius reports that Antony himself approved of this change in saying: "In the early days when I became a monk, there was no community for the nourishment of other souls; following the persecution, each of the early monks practiced asceticism on his own. But afterwards your father embarked upon this enterprise, with good effect, helped by the Lord."[22] The contrast implied in the words "on his own" and "community for the nourishment of other souls" is very strong. Monasticism, from its inception, understood the usefulness of community as both increasing the pressure for the monk to understand his own soul, and as providing support and encouragement for this task. And yet the rivalry between cenobitic and eremitic life-styles indicates that more was being argued than which style best advanced goals that both groups agreed upon. While all agreed that the ultimate goal was the service and love of God, they disagreed strongly on the immediate goals that led to it.

Out of the critique of the temptations of solitary life, monastic leaders, many of whom had themselves begun their spiritual lives as solitaries, evolved a new immediate goal for the monk, life in community. One's method intimately affects one's ultimate goal, and the early monastic leaders detected, in the hermit's lifelong absorption with his own soul, something like the sublimest form of self-seeking.[23] The importance of the right immediate goal is indicated in the statement of Abba Moses: "What is important is knowing where we ought to concentrate our mental attention and how to direct the eyes of the soul."[24] In life in community as the monastic writers conceived it, the hermits' quest for self-knowledge and self-mastery is not rejected but critiqued and incorporated in a context of service within and without the community.

The salvation of the monk in the community is a "fringe benefit" of his attention to the needs of others. Basil's *Rule* develops the implications of this concentration on practical charity. Rule 7, "It is both disagreeable and dangerous to live alone," contrasts the humility of attending to others to the self-preoccupation of the solitary. Benedict also, although his *Rule* does not condemn solitude, explicitly insists that the monk "persevere in the monastery until death."[25]

In the early monastic Rules there is a noticeable diminishing of interest in the standard ascetic "tools" of the desert hermit. If life in community is the immediate goal, ascetic feats lessen in value. Gone is the tone of competition or rivalry we find in Palladius' *Lausiac History* or in some of the apothegms. These are undesirable and divisive qualities in a community. "Corporal austerity brings the first beginnings of progress," John Cassian wrote, "but it does not beget that perfect charity which has the promise of this life and the life to come."[26]

Cassian's *Conferences,* which describe the wisdom of some of the desert hermits with whom Cassian spoke during his ten-year visit to Egypt, represents both the characteristic veneration of these "athletes" and also the belief that whatever the solitaries could do, monastics could do better. Life in community is in all respects better able to "cure" the vices of "anger, gloom, and impatience" which concern the solitary hermit:

> For curing the faults I have been talking about, human society, so far from being a hindrance, is useful. The more often people see that they are impatient, the more thoroughly they do penitence and the more rapidly they achieve a sound mind.

The only two practices retained by Basil are "withdrawal from the world" and silence.[27] Desert hermits left the "world" to concentrate on the perfection of their souls, but in the early monastic movement such withdrawal changes in significance. What can the monastic achieve that the person in the world cannot? What is the significance of the retreat itself from the secular world?

The answer to these questions lies in the insights of early monastic authors into the nature and structure of secular society. To the monk, the social structure of the secular world consisted of the management of the three powerful instincts of sex, power, and possession. Monks saw that although secular culture claims to govern these and thus minimize conflicts that would endanger society, these instincts are essentially concupiscence, the direction of infinite human longing to the possession of objects which, though good in themselves, cannot fulfill such longing. Secular culture both provides conditions for the pursuit of sex, power, and possessions and limits the destructiveness of infinite demand. The fact that secular culture oriented and organized life around these instincts makes it pervasively corrupt.

Monastic life, then, was a counter culture. In it, instincts of sex, power, and possession were consciously sacrificed in a rejection of secular culture. That *more* life is the object of such sacrifice is clear from monastic writings. The prologue to Benedict's *Rule* conceives the call to monastic life as simply a call to *"life"*:

> Dearest brethren, can we imagine anything more tender than this invitation of our Lord? See, in his goodness, he points out to us the way of life.

Life is gained by rejecting instinctual satisfactions. Instead of the pursuit of sex, the monk vows celibacy; instead of the pursuit of power, he vows obedience; instead of seeking possessions, he vows poverty. With these vows he rejects the deadening agenda of secular culture: "The Scripture awakens us saying, 'Now it is the hour to arise from sleep.'"

The monastic solution to the agenda of instinct is the core of the monastic life. The community is formed by adherence to a counter culture based on obedience, poverty, and chastity. Each of the early Rules carefully articulates both the negative aspect of these rejections and the positive affirmation of their opposites, the monastic virtues.

> The absolute unquestioning obedience of the monk is strongly stressed: The first degree of humility is a prompt and ready obedience. *This is fitting for them who love Christ above all else.* . . . They make no more delay to comply, the very instant anything is appointed them, than if God himself had given the command. . . . They who are of this temper abandon all, even to their very will; instantly clear their hands, and leave unfinished what they had begun; so that the command is carried out in the moment it is uttered.[28]

The *Rule* of St. Benedict even gives instruction for circumstances in which a brother is ordered to do something "impossible":

> If a brother is ordered to do something difficult or impossible he shall receive the order with good temper and submission. If he sees that it is altogether beyond his power, he may patiently wait an opportunity to show his superior why it is impossible, provided he do it in a humble and not in a rebellious spirit. If, notwithstanding his plea, the superior persists in the order, the brother is to be persuaded that it is for his good, and in charity, trusting in God's help, shall obey.[29]

But who is strong enough to command absolute obedience without becoming addicted to power? Benedict's careful description of the balance of power in the monastery acknowledges that this is a problem if the "world" is not to be brought into the monastery in an unconscious way. First, the brothers are to obey one another. Since "obedience of its own nature is a thing so good that . . . by way of this obedience they will come to God," all forms of it are intrinsically useful. The abbot, however, ultimately retains the responsibility of accepting the obedience of all the monks and using it for the salvation of their souls:

> Let the abbot always remember that on the dreadful day of judgment he is accountable for the obedience of his disciples as for his own teaching.

Obedience is thus deflected back into the community and is not to be seen as coming to rest in the person of the abbot. Also, the abbot is chosen, not for secular reasons of seniority, but "for the goodness of his life and the excellence of his wisdom, even though he be the last in the house according to seniority."[30] Election, then, is a "weighty burden," rather than an honor. The abbot's care for every physical and spiritual aspect of the life of his monks is emphasized in a way which strongly qualifies the office of the abbot when *obedience* is at issue. The abbot, in order to compensate for the absolute obedience he receives from the monks, is instructed not to exaggerate his authority but to "endeavor much more to be loved than feared."[31]

As an operational check on the abbot's exercise of power, Benedict urges that the whole community be involved in making necessary decisions. Not only does the consultation of the community formally underscore the abbot's role of service, but consultation is important in that an unlikely member of the community may possess wisdom on the matter at hand that the abbot should receive with gratitude:

> We have for this reason ordained that the whole community should be assembled, because God often reveals what is best to the young.

Secondly, the possession of personal property is discussed by Benedict as the most pernicious of all vices:

> The vice of possessing property is particularly to be banished from the monastery.
> No one may presume to give or receive anything without the abbot's leave, or to possess anything whatever, not even book or tablets or pen. The monks' bodies and their wills are not at their own disposal. They must look to all their needs to be supplied by the common father of the monastery.[32]

Finally, monastic discipline took for granted the necessity of chastity. The demand for chastity was a way of reinforcing the monastic emphasis on the alternative community—the spiritual community. No rationale is offered for celibacy in the Rules of the fifth and sixth centuries, but its usefulness was never questioned. Clearly marriage and parenthood represented investments in the secular community that were the exact antithesis of monastic "withdrawal." Even the potential distraction of the "lusts of the flesh" is secondary to the encroachment on loyalty to the monastic community that sexual relationship would entail. For the monk, sexual activity both threatened the community and committed the individual to the structure of secular society.

In summary, the monastic Rules describe a new understanding of the failure of the secular world to orient human beings to "life" and provide an alternative community. Monastic writers consider participation in the communal life of the Kingdom of God as brothers rather than as rivals, a powerful irruption of eternal life into the present. Benedict describes the goal of the monastic sacrifice in the Prologue of his *Rule*:

> As we advance in the practices of religion and in faith, the heart insensibly opens and enlarges through the wonderful sweetness of his love, and we run in the way of God's commandments. If we then keep close to our school and the doctrine we learn in it . . . we shall here share by patience in the passion of Christ and hereafter deserve to be united with him in his kingdom.

III

A third historical model of the functions and goals of asceticism is St. Augustine. Augustine's mature treatises on ascetic practices emphasize the gathering and focusing of energy. They demonstrate the results of Augustine's lifelong effort at integrating the human body on the metaphysical level. The ascetical treatises are not themselves metaphysical, but rather assume the theological understanding that led Augustine to insist that the body is a primary *condition* of the soul's learning. This view of the body as condition makes Augustine's recommendation of ascetic practices consistent. The body was neither a problem nor a foil when he wrote of asceticism.

To view the body as a problem, for Augustine, was to emphasize its "weakness," that is, its susceptibility to disease and pain and its inevitable death:

> We make up this whole: the flesh itself, which dies when the soul departs, is our weak part, and is not dismissed as to be fled from, but is placed aside to be received again, and when it is received, it will be abandoned no more.[33]

The view of the body as the "weak" part does not require, however, the practice of asceticism. Augustine repeatedly insisted in his treatise on continence that a Christian must not practice asceticism in order to punish the body for its instability and ultimate insubordination in death. Rather, the soul alone has been dissipated and has become the source of incontinence. It is the soul which needs to be strengthened. Ascetic practices are not to be directed *against* the body, but must depend gratefully on the body to bring about spiritual benefit. This model relies very heavily on the *connection* of body and soul in which the body is a condition:

> The body is by nature certainly different than the soul, but it is not alien to the nature of human beings. The soul is not made up of the body, but

human beings are made up of soul and body, and surely, whom God sets free, he sets free as a whole person. For this reason the Savior himself assumed a whole human nature, freeing in us the whole that he had made.[34]

The body as foil, commonplace in late classical popular thought, was equally unacceptable to Augustine as a rationale for asceticism. Arguing against this position, he wrote:

You consider the flesh as fetters, but who loves his fetters? You consider the flesh a prison, but who loves his prison? . . . No matter how great a master of the flesh you may be, and no matter how great may be the severity toward the flesh with which you are kindled, I am inclined to think that you will close your eye if any blow threatens it.[35]

If, then, the body is the condition of the soul's learning, what ascetic practices does Augustine recommend as useful? Such practices are not, for Augustine, good things in themselves, but, consistent with his definition of the soul as the life of the body, he considers the conversion of the soul's energy to "that which truly and supremely is"[36] and away from preoccupation with the body a highly valuable goal. To this end, Augustine recommends only celibacy—a gift of God not to be enforced by "willpower"—and fasting, which he finds incontestably "useful," as described in his treatise *De utilitate jejunii,* "The Usefulness of Fasting."

While it is clearly not the body but the soul's care for it that dissipates the soul's energy, Augustine describes ascetic practices as methods of rebalancing the soul's weight of love. If the soul's constant flow of energy into the body and the external world remains unchecked, it will expend itself totally. To elaborate on his vision of the soul's investment in the agenda of the body, Augustine uses language confusing in its apparent disregard of his preference for viewing the body as condition. He refers, for example, to the "usefulness of fasting" as "cheating the flesh" for the "enrichment of the mind." We will consider later whether this is adequate in the light of Augustine's own statement that the soul's *first* duty is the care of its body. And yet when Augustine considers the psychology of fasting, we can see clearly the direct connection he assumes between a bodily and a psychic condition:

When people are hungry, they stretch out toward something; while they are stretching they are enlarged; while they are enlarged they become capacious, and when they have become capacious enough, they will be filled in due time.[37]

This is not a "cheating of the flesh to enrich the mind," but the cultivation of a physical condition which creates that same condition in the soul. States of the body become conditions of the soul. The soul's learning cannot be effected by contemplation alone, but requires a bodily condition of exacerbated appetite to increase the soul's longing and capacity.

Yet when Augustine examines the mechanics of ascetic practices, his model is nonetheless that of "cheating the flesh to enrich the soul":

Why, therefore, is it of benefit to us to abstain somewhat from food and carnal pleasure? The flesh draws one to the earth. The mind tends upwards; it is caught up by love, but it is slowed down by weight.[38]

The metaphor of weight suddenly becomes the literal body weight as opposed to the soul's own "weight." "My weight is my love," Augustine wrote in *Confessions* XIII.9. The soul's "weight" is indistinguishably part of the body's weight, which "pins" the soul to loving care for the body.

But the body can only become its "best" in an enlarged soul, and the soul is only able to achieve this by withdrawing its attention from the body and the external world. The soul can then begin to be aware of its own potential: "The soul in every way forms a conception of how great it is, and having conceived this, it proceeds with incredibly powerful confidence toward God, that is, to the real contemplation of truth."[39] It is only from the new vantage point of "incredibly powerful confidence" that the soul can give to its body, its "spouse," as Augustine calls it in *City of God* XV.7, the surcharge of vitality by which the body is made a permanent participant in the unique property of the soul, life.

Before the soul's temporary and partial withdrawal from the body for purposes of "coming to itself," its relationship to the body, as described by Augustine, is such that

the soul quickens by its presence this earthly and mortal body, it gathers it into one and holds it in one, it does not allow it to fall apart and decay; it causes food to be distributed equally among the members of the body, allotting to each what is proper to it; it preserves its harmony and measure, not only in beauty of form, but also in growth and reproduction.[40]

After the soul's gathering and strengthening, its greater participation in life extends to the body:

But perfect health of body shall be the ultimate immortality of the whole person. For God has endowed the soul with a nature so powerful that from

utter fullness of joy which is promised to the saints at the end of time,
there overflows also over the lower part of our nature, which is the body,
. . . plenitude of health, that is to say, the vigor of incorruption.[41]

The whole purpose of ascetic practice, then, is that the soul may win a
temporary reprieve from its constant care of the body. That ascetic
practices accomplish this goal was both a commonplace of late classical
thought and an experiential fact for Augustine. We must honor his
description of his conversion to celibacy as one of being freed from the
compulsive sexuality which had focused his attention and energy.

In the practices Augustine advocates, celibacy and fasting, we see two
different ideas of what asceticism can do and why it is necessary.
Celibacy, as he tells us in *Confessions,* was a "final solution" to the
hegemony of sex. Fasting, on the other hand, makes the soul
"capacious." Although Augustine never tells us how a bodily condition
can effect a condition of the soul, he yet understood the body to be, quite
literally, the *condition* of the soul's enrichment.

IV

The fourth model of the methods and goals of ascetic practice is the
Spiritual Exercises of Ignatius Loyola. In 1521, Ignatius, Basque
nobleman, soldier, courtier, and carefree adventurer, received a leg
wound in a border skirmish and went to Loyola to recuperate. The only
reading matter available to him included collections of saints' lives and
Ludolph of Saxony's *Life of Christ.* Ignatius occupied himself in reading
these books with his characteristic enthusiasm. Convinced of the need
for reform of his life, he set out on a pilgrimage to Jerusalem, but stopped
at Manresa, a small town on the way to Barcelona, where he stayed for
ten months to concentrate on organizing the life of his spirit. During this
time he wrote down whatever he found useful, and his book, the
Spiritual Exercises, part of which came from this and part from a later
period, describes the way he arrived at his extraordinary spiritual
experiences at Manresa and also suggests a method for others to use, a
carefully graded program of the spiritual life.

The *Exercises* became the basis for the new spirituality of the Jesuit
priest, a highly energized integration of personal experience and an
individualized method of interpreting that experience, incorporating as
well absolute obedience to a spiritual director. The tremendous pastoral
efficiency of Jesuit priests was immediate evidence of the effectiveness

of the *Exercises*. It is hard for us to imagine how shocking this spirituality must have been in its own time. It rejected many traditional features of monasticism: the chanting of the daily hours of the divine office, special dress, and all compulsory ascetic practices. Jesuits were encouraged *not* to mortify their bodies to excess by fasting, loss of sleep, or whatever might harm their studies or their activities of service and missionary endeavor. Ignatius' vision was not of a spiritual athlete perpetually exploring the inner reaches of the psyche, nor of the monk with attention focused on the community, but of the missionary priest, effectively integrated for loving service.

Ignatius did not want introspection to be a time-consuming and permanent occupation for a priest. He preferred a method that would rapidly, and with minimal maintenance, concentrate consciousness so that a choice of vocation could be made from the perspective of awareness of one's characteristic weaknesses, difficulties, affinities, and strengths. Once this choice was made, the person could devote undiluted energy and commitment to loving service. Ignatius' instructions in the *Exercises* describe a short, intensive period of concentrated introspection for a specific purpose.

The self of the *Exercises* is the phenomenal self, crusty with habit, deadened by habituation to food, sleep, and attention to practical daily concerns, the "inordinate attachments" which must not be permitted to influence one's vocational decisions.[42] The prescription for overcoming the phenomenal self is a series of mental and physical exercises that effectively break both habitual thought patterns and habitual treatment of the body. These can then be reintegrated in more productive directions, the body in more conscious management of physical needs, the mind in love of God and service to others.

The *Exercises* were not written to be read, they were to be given by a spiritual director in the context of a retreat from daily life. The director, not the client, was responsible for tailoring both the length and the content of the exercises to the spiritual needs of the individual.[43] This combination of obedience on the part of the exercitant and sensitivity on the part of the director created an atmosphere of tension that strongly focused the former's attention.

Two techniques dominate the *Exercises*, employed at the discretion of the director: directed meditation and "penances." Both techniques assume the mutual interdependence of soul and body and definitely involve the latter. Both intensify consciousness. Meditation is strengthened by instruction in "visualizations," and penances are, according to the requirements of the individual, stronger ascetic practices than any we have seen advocated in the models we have already examined.

The directed meditations aim not at "an abundance of knowledge" but at "an interior understanding and savoring of things," an *experience* that can effect a lasting reorientation. It is impossible to read the *Exercises* without comparing them to the far less skillful popular psychological "retreats" of our time. The similarities are striking, but so are the differences. The most noticeable differences are (1) there is no attempt on the part of the director to structure and manipulate a transference of dependence to himself; (2) there is no exploration or interest in the "sins" of the client by the director;[44] and (3) no one is encouraged to adopt a particular vocation or life-style.[45]

Visualization is the main technique for strengthening meditation. The exercitant does not merely think but minutely reconstructs images that place the thoughts within a concrete landscape. The imagination is fully drawn into meditation rather than repressed. The format is made up of the events of Christ's earthly life. These are the "places" the psyche is located in and bonded to, the "places" of Christ's life.

> To form a mental image of the scene and see in my imagination the road from Nazareth to Bethlehem. I will consider its length and breadth, and whether it is level or winding through valleys or over hills. I will also behold the place of the cave of the Nativity, whether it is large or small, whether high or low, and what it contains.[46]

It is not only visualizations which draw the imagination into meditation, but the employment of all the senses in imagination: the smell and taste of the event, the sound of the spoken words, the texture of the objects in the scene. All enrich the sense of being there and create total participation in the events of Christ's life. Thus, the pains and joys of the individual are placed in a paradigmatic setting and removed from their phenomenal, accidental, particular setting as random personal experiences. The sensory imaginings that accompany the meditations are crucial to this placing of the individual's most intimate experience in the life of Christ.

Finally, the physical positions and practices that accompany the meditations were carefully analyzed by Ignatius in terms of what they contribute to the concentration of consciousness. Here a curious fact emerges. Since Ignatius attempted to construct a strongly expanded and intensified consciousness in a short period of time, ascetic practices were increased in order to effect this. He recognized the effectiveness of deprivation of sleep and food for altering the psyche, but he also counseled inflicting pain on the body. Thus he expected to center consciousness sharply on making life choices based not on "inordinate affection" but on self-knowledge and identification with the life of Christ. Whatever judgment we may wish to make of this method must start from a recognition of its *effectiveness*. For example, if one, while cutting vegetables and with many unconnected thoughts flowing aimlessly through the mind, inadvertently cuts a finger, the "stream of consciousness" is immediately broken, and the whole attention of the person is turned to the pain of the moment. Ignatius did not consider minor harm to the body too high a price for a concentrated consciousness:

> To help the exercitant make the exercises better and to assist him in finding what he desires . . . by chastising the flesh, thereby causing sensible pain. This is done by wearing hair shirts, cords, or iron chains on the body, or by scourging or wounding oneself, or by other kinds of austerities.
>
> What seems the most suitable and safest thing in doing penance is for the pain to be felt in the flesh, without penetration to the bones, thus causing pain but not illness. Therefore it seems more fitting to scourge oneself with light cords, which cause exterior pain, than in another way which causes internal infirmity.[47]

We should note that these instructions *permit* rather than promote such practices. Their use was always a part of the *Exercises* designed by the director in accordance with the temperament and condition of the individual, permitted because their effectiveness was a commonplace in Ignatius' world. If the question we are exploring as we look at these models of the value of ascetic practice is what *these* people thought they were doing, then we must grant them the validity of the methods they found effective. The ruthless search for the truth of one's life must be honored, however much others may reject the methods employed in the search.

During the four weeks of the exercises, the individual is moved by the director through the range of emotional states of the psyche. During the first week, one concentrates on one's personal burden of sin—or *guilt*, as we today prefer to call the recognition of one's failures. In the first week, this burden is purposely evoked in all its frightening potential to overwhelm the psyche. The director is alert to this danger and prepared to avert it:

If the Master of the *Exercises* sees that the exercitant is in desolation or tempted, he should be careful not to be severe or harsh with him but rather gentle and kind. He should give him courage and strength for the future, helping him to see the wiles of the enemy of our human nature, and having him prepare and dispose himself for consolation to come.[48]

But during this stage, despite the director's sensitivity to the need for the exercitant to be reminded of "consolation to come," the individual is encouraged to remain in a dark room and to repress thoughts that rationalize or modify the awareness of sin:

I will strive not to permit myself any joyful thoughts, even though they are good and holy, as are those of the resurrection and the glory of heaven. I will rather rouse myself to sorrow, suffering and deep pain, frequently calling to mind the labors, burdens, and sufferings that Christ our Lord bore from the moment of his birth up to the mystery of his passion, which I am now contemplating.[49]

This meditation visualizes the places where one lived and one's friends and job[50] in order to re-create the conditions in which the sin can be relived, but now in its appropriate setting, hell. As long as sins are defended by habit and protected by rationalization, one never sees them in this setting. They are, Ignatius instructs, to be seen in their context, "the length, breadth, and depth of hell."[51]

By gathering and reliving one's sins, the retreatant is relieved of repressing or rationalizing the destructive effects of sin on oneself and on others—something that is among the most closely guarded burdens of every human being. Ignatius then advises taking on one's own punishment as the natural outcome of the "interior penance" of recognizing and acknowledging sins. While we may not find this idea attractive—and we will look more carefully later at why we do not—I think we must acknowledge that it was valid and useful for people of Ignatius' time, to whom awareness of their sins may have been difficult to achieve. Sixteenth-century people, we must remember, were not post-Freudians. For them, an awareness of the mechanics of destructive behavior was not a cultural inheritance.

Two weeks of contemplating the earthly life and passion of Christ are followed by contemplation of the resurrection. Having lived through the pain, guilt, and despair of the dark season of the psyche, the person can now completely experience the joyousness of the resurrection. Just as no modifying thoughts or physical surroundings were to interfere with the reliving of one's pain in a cosmic setting, so now no awareness of the dark side of the psyche is to interfere with the participation of mind and senses in the joy of resurrection. Only when the darkness and pain have been entered and experienced to the full can full pleasure and delight be experienced.

> Upon waking, I will see in my mind's eye the contemplation that I am about to make and I will strive to feel joy and gladness at the great joy and gladness of Christ our Lord; . . . to occupy my thoughts with things that cause pleasure, happiness, and spiritual joy, for example the thought of heaven; . . . to take advantage of the light and the comforts of the season, for example, the refreshing breezes of spring and summer, and the warmth of the sun and of a fire in winter.[52]

The love of God which creates the heaven of the soul is also visualized: "Here it is to see how I stand in the presence of God our Lord and of the angels and saints, who intercede for me."[53]

The method of the *Exercises*, then, is an analysis of psychic contents and aims to subvert the automatic balance of pain and joy ordinarily constructed by us in daily consciousness. The unmodified, extreme states of the psyche, fully "exercised," will then lend their energy to the conscious choices made by the retreatant. The decisions that emerge will bear the assent of the *whole* psyche; they will not be decisions made for one part of it by another.

VII

TOWARD A NEW ASCETICISM

ARE WE MISSING SOMETHING because of our insistence that ascetic practice is a psychological "sickness" disavowing the human body? If any of historical asceticism's goals attracts us, if one or more of these goals concern us as individuals or as a culture, then we must, I think, take seriously the claim of historic authors that ascetic practices are the best means toward them.

If learning to understand and change one's basing of choices on unconscious patterns of attraction or repulsion is important to us, and if we find that the ascetics of the Egyptian desert were remarkably skillful at just this task, then we must acknowledge the extent to which ascetic practices supported their endeavor.

If one of our priorities is to locate our cultural conditioning so as consciously either to act out of this conditioning or to begin to modify it; and if we see that monasticism was a creative and skillful resolution of precisely this social conditioning, so that men and women were able to make choices in the direction of more love and more life than their cultural options offered, then we must recognize that the asceticism advocated by monastic authors was essential to achieving freedom from that conditioning.

If gathering and focusing energy in a culture increasingly given to distraction and entertainment is a primary concern for us, and if we see that historic thinkers like Augustine, who lived in cultures similar in this respect to our own, were able to effect this concentration and direction of energy, then we must be prepared to consider carefully the ascetic methods they found most useful.

If we value the intensification and concentration of consciousness in order to make life choices in the conscious context of our *whole* lives as well as in our historical and cosmic context, and if we think that, far from being a modern notion, this was well known, often described, and highly valued by historic authors like Ignatius Loyola, then we must ask ourselves whether methods they used to achieve this might not be useful to us also.

Although we may, on these historical recommendations, acknowledge the usefulness of some form of bodily discipline, we may still be uneasy about the bases on which historic authors often advocate asceticism. Again and again we have found the idea of a closed energy system in which the soul gathers energy at the expense of the body: "When the soul grows strong, the body withers; when the body grows strong, the soul withers."[1] One of the desert ascetics put this even more strongly: "I am killing it because it is killing me."[2] This offends us because of its identification of the "I" in the domineering soul, and because it echoes descriptions of dualistic conflict within the human person subscribed to by many ascetic authors in the Western tradition.

How can we understand statements like these in the light of a Christian tradition which teaches that participation in the source of life irreducibly and permanently includes the human body? Although we can recognize the reasonableness of distinguishing between competition for energy and attention within a closed energy system, and the idea that to be human is to be composed of antagonistic components, this does not render any more acceptable the God/world and soul/body dichotomies we so often find in Christian asceticism. Augustine's principles of "cheating the flesh" to "enrich the mind"[3] clearly assumes a closed energy system implying no antagonism between "flesh" and "mind," yet in *tone* it suggests such an antagonism. We must reject rationales for ascetic practice that are inconsistent with the Christian affirmation of the human body by the doctrines of creation, incarnation, and resurrection.

Another common rationale for ascetic practice is also disturbing. Augustine's defense of fasting was quoted as a principle by medieval authors to the time of Ignatius Loyola: "I will punish myself so that he will spare me; I will take vengeance on myself so that he may come to my aid."[4] Although conscious attempts to expiate one's guilt may be psychologically sound, it seems presumptuous to take control of one's own judgment and punishment. We can see the value of making conscious one's sense of guilt and finding ways to acknowledge and relieve it, yet punitive asceticism still seems far more negative than positive. As a rationale for ascetic practice we must reject it.

These two major difficulties of the "old asceticism" are severe enough to have persuaded us as individuals and as a culture that asceticism is without value for us. And yet we know all too well about seizing the vitality and energy of the body for purposes of the psyche. Because the contemporary version of the "old asceticism" differs from its historical antecedents, we have not recognized the old asceticism in our lives. We live our lives at a pace that constantly requires us to "have" experiences which we have no leisure to make *our* own. We live in cities with more asphalt than green growth and with a noise level that fatigues us to a degree which we recognize only when we take the time to drive for an hour or two to somewhere quiet enough to hear the birds singing. We breathe polluted air, and if we run or cycle, we breathe even more of it than if we drive or walk. Our values require us to live and work in city environments, but often we have neither recognized nor acknowledged the sacrifice we make for them, the sacrifice of living in a gentler, more rhythmic, and more nurturing natural environment. These sacrifices, unclaimed and unused, can be nothing more than unconscious masochism in contemporary life, the precise opposite of the "asceticism" they can become if we recognize that we make them for delight in our work and in participation with other human beings in coming to know ourselves and our world.

But the asceticism of our lives in crowded, noisy, polluted environments is mild compared to the misuse of the body's energy and vitality evident in such prevalent practices in our culture as alcoholism, promiscuity, drug dependence, overeating, and overwork. Why have we not noticed that self-indulgence is the new guise of the "old asceticism" in our time? These practices, which harm the body and may even on occasion cause premature death, are rightly called masochistic.

We must reject the "old asceticism," whether we find it in historical rationales for ascetic practices or disguised as self-indulgence in contemporary culture. But the historic authors we have examined here present another model for asceticism that may be much more fruitful for us. The more careful ascetic authors describe a dialectic, not of mind (or soul) and body, but of those aspects of the human being distinguished as "spirit" and "flesh." This is Scriptural language, and it sets the human being either in the perspective of connection to the source of life and being, or in that of the disorientation caused by clutching at objects of immediate pleasure and enjoyment. Such objects, good in themselves, become "too dear" in that the person becomes attached to them instead of to the source of life and being. They become addictive. Because they are created things that owe their being to the generosity of the Creator, they cannot provide the infinite life and satisfaction for which human beings long. We are addicted when we refuse to recognize that we demand of these objects what they cannot provide. We need to recognize that forcing them beyond their capacity to give devalues them, and that we must continually be frustrated by their inability to give us greater life.

Christian tradition followed Paul's analysis of the human condition in calling this desperate and unconscious demand "the flesh." The body is a prize that the spirit and the flesh must struggle to possess. The flesh, strengthened by its daily exercise, becomes—they saw—automatically powerful and usually gains control of the body, easily asserting over the body its agenda of sex, power, and possession. The agenda of the flesh is hard on the body and the soul, inflicting the anxiety that at any moment its objects of desire will fail to provide the large and real emotion constantly required for feeling fully alive. If, however, the spirit is consciously strengthened by exercise appropriate to it, and by self-knowledge and orientation to the source of life, the spirit can take possession of the body. And possession of the body by the spirit is in all ways, and not just with regard to ultimate resurrection, good for the body. The body, connected to its source of life through possession by the spirit, suffers no inertia, no "sluggishness," and can already begin to participate in the life of the resurrection.

Ascetic practice can make sense as a way to ease the grasp of the flesh on the body. It is directed to the "flesh," not to the body. It is a method to break the hegemony of the flesh over the body so that the spirit, hitherto uncultivated, unexercised, and unstrengthened, can begin to possess it. Neither discipline nor punishment is the goal of asceticism, but rather freeing of the body from the stranglehold of the flesh so that it can come to share in the life and energy of the spirit.

Christian authors have often substituted the nontechnical language of "body" and "soul" for the more theological "flesh" and "spirit." Soul is then severely differentiated from body as the location of spirit, and body is carelessly identified with the flesh that possesses it. This language confuses and frustrates us by contradicting the metaphysical affirmation of the human body to which Christian authors are committed by Christian doctrine. The "old asceticism" is the result of a collapse of the Pauline language of spirit and flesh into that of soul and body. This distorts and caricatures the relation of soul and body because it maintains the antagonism between "spirit" as the connection with life and "flesh" as the deadening agenda of the soul.

Ascetic practice as a struggle for more life through strengthening the spirit's energizing control of the body is not an idea alien to us. In a society that features distraction and entertainment we are familiar with the need to gather and focus energy. We recognize also our need to make life choices based on accurate self-knowledge and oriented to love and service. We realize that we must identify and resolve our inner conflicts. We feel the longing to be "truly alive," and we are learning to look for deadness in precisely those aspects of experience identified by Christian tradition. Liberation theologies teach us to be suspicious of self-protective power structures. We are beginning to look at our own materialism and that of our culture, as well as our ways of constructing self-esteem. We are learning to recognize deadness in exploitive sexuality.

Some of us are more aware of these deadening agenda than others. Feminists, those of the second and third worlds (who are two thirds of the world's people), and those with sexual preferences not honored in their cultures all provide a critique of the reigning cultural styles of the pursuit of sex, power, and possessions. But to rearrange power structures, redistribute wealth, and recognize sexual affinities based on mutual love and protection is not enough. This must be done, but on the recognition that neither arrangements nor rearrangements of sex, power, and possessions guarantee being "truly alive." It is because every human being is equidistant from the source of our individual and corporate life—God who is Life Itself—that we understand ourselves as under obligation to become conscious of, and to rectify, the forms of our life together.

These are great tasks for which we need to gather and focus our energy. If, as historic authors repeatedly said, ascetic practices are the most efficient "tool" for orienting ourselves to the source of our being and life and eliminating our deadness, what might a "new asceticism" for our time look like?

First, any rationale for ascetic practice must assume that the human body is permanently and integrally connected with the soul so that when the state of the body is changed by ascetic practice, the soul is affected and becomes liable to change. When the body retains the same state of nourishment and the same patterns of habit, the soul retains its habitual consciousness and its ironclad agenda, so protected that it is difficult or impossible even to detect what these agenda are.

Secondly, an asceticism for our time must consist of practices fully as good for body as for soul. The body as an integral and permanent aspect of the human being must be cared for and enhanced by any ascetic practice we accept as useful for our souls. We cannot commit ourselves to anything resembling the closed energy system model with its implication of antagonism between the two.

Thirdly, ascetic practices must be temporary, and individually designed to locate and correct particular debilitating addiction. They must, in other words, be directed to confront the unconscious, masochistic asceticisms in contemporary life that debilitate body *and* soul.

Finally, some ascetic practices remain perennially useful. Even a small experiment with fasting for one meal demonstrates to most of us the degree of our habituation to food, not only as our bodies require and enjoy it, but especially for organizing our days. One day's fasting can provide an astonishingly different experience of time. In *The Magic Mountain*, Thomas Mann describes the management of time in a tuberculosis sanatorium: so that the day will not weigh oppressively on the patients, it is broken up every two or three hours by meals or snacks. Always either eating or looking forward to eating, patients find days, months, and even years passing rapidly unnoticed. To a lesser degree this principle operates in our lives as well. Altering our eating patterns, even briefly, both teaches us the depth of our attachment to food and to mealtimes and loosens that attachment so that it never again has quite the strength that it had when we were not conscious of it. And fasting is good for the body. Short fasts of one to three days allow the body to rest from the constant labor of metabolism. Bodies as well as souls are benefited by days of rest.

Another kind of fasting whose usefulness is unambiguous is fasting from the media. The perspective we gain by temporarily stopping the constant barrage of words and images in the media shows us to what extent our consciousness is shaped and governed by external manipulation of our attention.[5]

Disciplines of meditation and prayer involving techniques of breathing and posture can also be useful to gather and concentrate energy. Such practices, while not greatly emphasized in Christian asceticism, are nonetheless present in Eastern Orthodox, Dominican, and Jesuit meditative instruction.

We are also coming to know "the grace of the Creator in giving us a body," as Evagrius Ponticus put it, when we are aware that various forms of physical exercise affect what the desert ascetics called the "tone" of the soul, *tonos tēs psychēs*. We understand the value of even temporary periods of celibacy, of solitude, of concentration, of silence. Any of these forms of asceticism can at times be highly effective in identifying and treating deadness in soul and habituation in body.

Now that we have begun to construct a "new asceticism," we should remember that asceticism aimed at mutual enrichment of soul and body is not a "new" idea. The Egyptian desert masters cautioned their disciples to care for their bodies and not let them, like a neglected coat, "fall into tatters."[6] Athanasius likewise described how Antony emerged from the inner desert after twenty years of austerities with "the same appearance of body as before."[7] We have also seen that the ascetic practices of monks and hermits alike were individually designed to address particular temptations at particular times. We have observed that the only exception to the temporary nature of these practices was celibacy, a permanent feature in the ascetic life.[8] Not even this, however, was unanimous: various historic authors from Clement of Alexandria to John Calvin urged marriage as an ascetic discipline. Clement wrote that the value of marriage lies in its capacity to expose temptations to impatience, temper, and self-seeking.[9] Calvin, taking this further than anyone else, considered celibacy a naturally temporary condition and marriage as an equivalent condition for spiritual progress:

> Let no one rashly despise marriage as something unprofitable or superfluous to him; let no one long for celibacy unless he can live without a wife. Also let him not provide in this state for the repose and convenience of the flesh, but only that, freed of this marriage bond, he may be more prompt and ready for all the duties of piety. And *since this blessing is conferred on many persons only for a time,* let every one abstain from marriage only so long as he is fit to observe celibacy. If his power to tame lust fails him, let him recognize *that the Lord has now imposed the necessity of marriage on him.*[10]

Finally, we have seen that the Christian authors who described the ascetic life of the fourth and fifth centuries were aware that fascination with the "tools" of the ascetic life can be both physically and spiritually enervating. Ascetic practices are *methods*, not goals. This is an important qualification, not only for historical asceticism, but also for a "new asceticism." Abba Moses, in Cassian's *Conferences*, described these practices as a method of reaching an immediate goal which itself is but a means toward our ultimate goal:

The ultimate goal of our way of life is, as I have said, the kingdom of God or kingdom of heaven. The immediate aim is purity of heart. For without purity of heart none can enter into that kingdom. We should fix our gaze on this target, and walk towards it in as straight a line as possible. If our thoughts wander away from it even a little, we should bring back our gaze towards it, and use it as a kind of test, which at once brings all our efforts back onto the one path.[11]

Our fascination with historical asceticism has often restricted itself to the ascetic practices themselves. The more dramatic practices have caught our attention enough to distract us from asking what their purposes were. Ascetic treatises seldom give details of the mechanics of asceticism because of the individuality of these and their intermediate status. The authors were fascinated by the "kingdom of God," not by the ascetic means to it.

The immediate goals of asceticism, once again, include self-understanding, overcoming of habituation and addiction, gathering and focusing of energy, ability to change our cultural conditioning, and intensification or expansion of consciousness. These are all aspects of what Abba Moses called "purity of heart." We, like the historical people who developed methods of asceticism to actualize these immediate goals, should not forget that the ultimate goal of Christian asceticism is "the kingdom of heaven."

Fasting, watching, meditation on Scripture, nakedness and poverty are not perfection, but the means toward it; not the end of our discipline but the means to that end. The person who is content with these practices as the *summum bonum,* and not as means, will use them in vain.[12]

There is a great deal of "new asceticism," as we have defined it, in historic sources, and there is a great deal of the "old asceticism" in contemporary life. Among the bewildering array of rationales for asceticism offered by historic authors, at least some authors describe the principles we have referred to as the "new asceticism." Recognizing this helps us—in the phrase of H. R. Niebuhr—to "remember what we have forgotten, and to appropriate as our own past much that seemed alien to us."[13] It also supports, encourages, and comforts us in our own struggle. Historic Christians too wanted to keep themselves oriented to the source of life, to life itself.[14] They found they could not do this through insight alone but also needed ways to work with the whole human being, body and soul. These simple, humble ways included helpful bodily practices. We, in our fascination with intellectual insight, often forget that to be Christian is to affirm an incarnational orientation to life whereby what we *do* is as important as what we *think*.

Historical study imparts a vision of our individual and collective past. Our times have been particularly attracted to Freud's "talking cure," the research and recovery of personal history and through it the formulation of a "case history" that describes us to ourselves. The insights gained in this way can cause change, change in the direction of feeling, of being more fully alive. But we have often assumed that the insights that enabled historic persons to live "blessed" lives are those formulated in Christian doctrine. In many ways, they are. But to focus exclusively on doctrinal insights is to neglect the perception of those authors that insight comes only after change, from *doing* differently.

Asceticism is only one aspect of personal change discussed in Christian history. True, asceticism was, in some notorious instances, shamefully misused, but this does not license us to caricature it as against life or masochistic. If we take seriously the admonition that changes in the habits and condition of the body open the soul to greater insight, we understand the need for a new asceticism. We too find ourselves cluttered with habits and addictions that deaden our sense of lifefulness. Historic authors variously named this loss of the sense of our connection to the source of all things "sluggishness," "fatigue of body," "inertia," "torpor," "dullness of apprehension," "smallness of soul," and "indifference," to name only a few. Christian asceticism is about more life, and the elimination of the deadness. The historic sources unanimously insist that ascetic practices are neither goods nor ends in themselves, nor do they merely divide the world of objects for us into good and bad objects. Ascetic practices that meet the requirements of a new asceticism can become valuable tools for contemporary Christians who, like historic Christians, could express our central longing in the prayer of Serapion of Thmuis, "We beg you, make us truly alive."

NOTES

INTRODUCTION

1. Tertullian, *De resurrectione carnis* 8. *Tertullian's Treatise on the Resurrection*, tr. by Ernest Evans (London: S.P.C.K., 1960), p. 25.

2. A. Meredith, "Asceticism—Christian and Greek," *Journal of Theological Studies*, Vol. XXVII, No. 2 (Oct. 1976).

3. Augustine, *De moribus ecclesiae catholicae* I.5.7 (Migne, *Patrologia Latina* 32).

4. See Descartes, *Fourth Replies, Letter to Newcastle,* and *Descriptions of the Human Body* XI, 224ff.

5. See the statement of the ascetic Abba Daniel, as reported in the fourth-century *apophthegmata* of the hermits of the Egyptian desert, as a typical statement of the dualism of much ascetic teaching: "If the body is strong, the soul withers. If the body withers, the soul is strong" (Owen Chadwick, ed., *Western Asceticism*, The Library of Christian Classics, Vol. XII; Westminster Press, 1958, p. 109).

I. MARTYRDOM, GNOSTICISM, AND THE EARLY CHURCH

1. Tertullian, *De resurrectione carnis* 7.

2. Ibid., 8.

3. *Barlaam and Joasaph*, ed. by Woodward and Mattingly (London: W. Heinemann, 1914). See also *Vita Antonii* 47: "Daily martyr to his conscience, ever fighting the battle of the faith."

4. Origen, *Hom. in Jerem.* IV.3.

5. *Letter to Diognetus* VII, in Cyril C. Richardson (ed.), *Early Christian Fathers*, The Library of Christian Classics, Vol. I (Westminster Press, 1953), p. 218.

6. Tertullian, *De carne Christi* v; see also vi.

7. Ibid., vi.

8. Ibid., x.

9. Ibid., xvii.

10. Ibid., iv.

11. Ibid.; see also Tertullian, *Adv. Marc.* iii.1; iv.21.

12. Tertullian, *De carne Christi* iv.

13. Tertullian, *De res.* 8.

14. Tertullian, *Apol.* 48.

15. Ibid.

16. Ibid., 110.

17. Tertullian, *De res.* 62; Matt. 22:30.

18. Tertullian, *De res.* 59.

19. Ibid., 60.

20. Ibid., 63.

21. Tertullian, *De spectaculis* 30.

22. A later Gnostic text, the Nag Hammadi *Treatise on the Resurrection,* describes such a view as Tertullian presents of the Gnostics' opinion of the resurrection in *De res.* 1-4.

23. Ibid., 3.

24. Ibid., 61: *"temporali vacatione."*

25. Ibid.: *"os (a) cibo excusamus."*

26. Ibid.: *"non desiderare."*

27. Irenaeus, *Adversus haereses* xxi.10.

28. Ibid., V.vi.i.

29. Ibid., III.xxii.1.

30. Ludwig Wittgenstein, *Tractatus Logico-Philosophicus,* 2d ed. (Harcourt, Brace and Co., 1933).

31. Irenaeus, *Adv. haer.* V.xvi.2.

32. Ibid., V.xii.4; see also V.xii.3.

33. Ibid., V.vi.1.

34. Ibid.

35. Ibid., III.xv.2.

36. Ibid., V.xi.2.

37. Ibid., V.xii.3.

38. Ibid., V.vii.2.

39. Ibid., V.xiv.4.

40. Ibid., V.xii.6.

41. Ibid., IV.xviii.5.

42. Ibid., V.xxiv ff.

43. Ibid., V.xxxii.1.

44. Ibid.

45. Ibid., IV.xviii.5.

46. Ibid., V.ii.3.

47. For a detailed discussion of the times and places of persecution of

Christians, see W. H. C. Frend, *Martyrdom and Persecution in the Early Church* (Oxford: Basil Blackwell, 1965).

48. Ignatius of Antioch, *To the Magnesians*, in Richardson, *Early Christian Fathers*, p. 95; *Didache*, ibid., p. 171.

49. Irenaeus, *Adv. haer.* IV.xx.6.

50. Origen, *Comm. in Ioannem* 1.37.

51. Origen, *Comm. in Matt.* xvi.8.

52. *The Letter of Polycarp, Bishop of Smyrna, to the Philippians*, in Richardson, *Early Christian Fathers*, p. 154.

53. Ibid., p. 156.

54. *The Martyrdom of Perpetua and Felicitas* in Anne Fremantle, *A Treasury of Early Christianity* (Viking Press, 1953), pp. 216ff.

55. *Polycarp, To the Philippians*, in Richardson, *Early Christian Fathers*, p. 154.

56. As described by Tertullian in *De spectaculis*.

57. Ignatius, *To the Romans*, in Richardson, *Early Christian Fathers*, p. 105.

58. Ibid., p. 104.

59. *Polycarp, To the Philippians*, in Richardson, *Early Christian Fathers*, p. 150.

60. *Letters from the Churches of Lyon and Vienne*, in Fremantle, *Treasury*, p. 210.

61. Ibid., p. 203.

62. Ibid., p. 210.

II. THE ORIGINS OF CHRISTIAN ASCETICISM

1. Frend, *Martyrdom and Persecution in the Early Church*, p. 356.

2. Clement, *Stromateis* VII.iii.16, in Henry Chadwick (ed.), *Alexandrian Christianity*, The Library of Christian Classics, Vol. II (Westminster Press, 1954), pp. 102f.

3. Ibid., VII.vii.35.

4. The negative view of the body as prison of the soul is presented in Plato, *Phaedo* 81b-e; the positive view appears in *Timaeus* 41e.

5. Clement, *Strom.* VII.ii.9.

6. Plato, *Ion* 533d-e.

7. Clement, *Strom.* VII.ii.10.

8. Ibid., VII.vii.48.

9. Ibid., VII.ii.11.

10. Ibid., VII.ii.10, 12.

11. Origen will treat this commonplace expression of the late classical world differently, beginning, not by refuting the "body as prison" view, but by asking himself in what sense it might be understood as accurate. See his *On First*

Principles 11.x.8; tr. by G. W. Butterworth (Peter Smith, 1973). See also his *Dialogue with Heraclides*, in H. Chadwick, *Alexandrian Christianity*.

12. Clement, *Strom.* III.v.40; all emphases in quotations are mine.

13. Ibid., VII.ii.60.

14. Ibid.

15. Ibid., III.v.41.

16. Ibid., III.xiv.95.

17. Ibid., VII.ii.9.

18. Ibid., III.iv.34.

19. Ibid., VII.x.63.

20. Clement does not offer to cite an example of his model human being, the "true gnostic." Like the early Stoics' frankly imaginative description of the "sage," there seems to be no fully appropriate living model! This, however, does not destroy the usefulness of a model toward which to strive. As the novelist Saul Bellow has remarked, "Greatness without models? Incomprehensible!"

21. Clement, *Strom.* VII.iii.14.

22. Ibid., VII.xi.61.

23. Ibid., VII.iii.13.

24. Ibid., VII.vii.40.

25. Ibid., VII.iii.19.

26. Ibid., VII.xvi.94.

27. Ibid., VII.iii.19.

28. Ibid., VII.x.57.

29. Ibid., III.iv.44.

30. Ibid., III.v.43.

31. Ibid., VII.ii.9.

32. Ibid., VII.iii.13.

33. Ibid.

34. Ibid., III.vii.103.

35. Ibid., VII.vii.40.

36. Ibid., III.xi.77.

37. Ibid., VII.vii.46.

38. Ibid., VII.vii.40.

39. Ibid., VII.ii.9.

40. Ibid., III.i.4.

41. Ibid., III. vi.47.

42. Ibid., III.vi.48.

43. Ibid., III.v.48; VII.vii.48.

44. Ibid., VII.xii.70. Whether or not this presents a "generous" view of marriage, it clearly presents a realistic one! It is even a view that may usefully critique our romantic view of marriage and indicate a correction for it. Clement's idea of marriage as spiritual discipline recasts the idea of "platonic love" (usually so completely misunderstood as nonsexual relationship). Platonic love is a

relationship of equals in which both parties encourage, support, and "egg each other on" to growth and understanding that neither could achieve alone (Plato, *Symposium* 210ff.).

45. Clement, *Strom.* VII.xii.70.

46. Col. 2:18, 23.

47. Clement, *Strom.* III.i.2; as the contemporary poet Robert Bly has so aptly said, "The point of spiritual labour is not to make you stiffer!"

48. Ibid., III.vii.57.

49. Ibid., III.vii.56.

50. Ibid., VII.xii.76.

51. Ibid., VII.xii.80; VII.xiii.81.

52. Origen, *Comm. in Ioannem* i.37, in Henry Bettenson, *The Early Christian Fathers* (Oxford University Press, 1956), p. 210.

53. Origen, *Exhortation to Martyrdom*, in H. Chadwick, *Alexandrian Christianity*, p. 394.

54. Origen, *Comm. in Matthaeum* xvi.8, in Bettenson, *The Early Christian Fathers*, p. 224.

55. Origen, *Dialogue*, pp. 454f.

56. Quoted in Henri de Lubac's Introduction to Origen, *On First Principles*, tr. by G. W. Butterworth (Peter Smith, 1973), p. xiii; hereafter referred to as *Prin.* First Published 1936. Quotations from this book are reprinted by permission of The Society for Promoting Christian Knowledge.

57. Origen, *Prin.* 11.xi.4, See also his *Exhortation*, in H. Chadwick, *Alexandrian Christianity*, p. 426: "But why did our Maker implant in us a longing for religious communion with him, so that even in the erring he preserves certain traces of the divine will, if it were not possible and attainable for rational beings to apprehend that which they long for by nature?"

58. Origen, *Prin.* I. Preface, 10.

59. Ibid., II.iv.4; IV.ii.1.

60. Ibid., III.i.17.

61. Origen, *In Matt. Comm.* Series 92, in Bettenson, *The Early Christian Fathers*, p. 219.

62. Origen, *Comm. Ep. ad Rom.* 1.18; see also his *Comm. in Ioannem* xxxii.18 and *Dialogue*, p. 441.

63. Origen, *Prin.* III.iv.2.

64. Ibid., III.iv.4.

65. Ibid.

66. Ibid., IV.iv.10.

67. Origen, *On Prayer*, in H. Chadwick, *Alexandrian Christianity*, pp. 272ff.

68. Origen, *Dialogue*, p. 448. Cf. Tertullian's statement of the opposite order of creation: "Man was first a clay figure, then an entire man," when God "breathed in his face the breath of life" (*De resurrectione carnis* 5).

69. Origen, *Prin.* I.vii.4.

70. Ibid., II.i.3, 4.

71. Ibid., II.i.4.

72. Origen, *Selecta in Psalmos,* Lommatzsch edition, xi, 384-391, in *Selections from the Commentaries and Homilies of Origen,* tr. by R. B. Tollinton (Macmillan Co. 1929), pp. 232f. See also Origen's *Contra Celsum* IV.lvii, in *The Ante-Nicene Fathers,* Vol. IV (Buffalo: Christian Literature Publishing Co., 1885).

73. Origen, *Prin.* III.vi.3.

74. Ibid., II.ii.2: "Now what else can this 'incorruption' and 'immortality' be except the wisdom and word and righteousness of God, which mould and clothe and adorn the soul."

75. Ibid., II.iii.2.

76. Ibid.

77. Origen, *Dialogue,* p. 442.

78. Origen, *Prin.* II.vi.3.

79. Ibid., II.ix.6; see also III.iv.2.

80. Ibid., II.x.8.

81. Ibid.; see also IV.iv.9.

82. Ibid., II.x.8.

83. Origen, *Super Isaiam.* Frag. *Pamphili Apologia* vii, in Tollinton, *Selections,* pp. 228-238.

84. Ibid., pp. 232f.; Cf. Plotinus' description of the merging at death of "all powers"—desire, feeling, and sensation—into "one soul," along with the *hegemonikon* or life principle itself (*Enneads* IV.ix.3; IV.iv.29).

85. Origen, *Prin.* II.iii.2.

86. Ibid., III.vi.4, 6; see also III.i.14.

87. Ibid., III.vi.5.

88. Ibid., I.i.7; see also I Peter 3:19; cf. Plotinus, *Enneads* IV.3.24: "Souls, body-bound, are apt to body punishment"; Plato, *Phaedrus* 250c; *Cratylus* 400c; *Phaedo* 81c.

89. Ibid., II.x.4.

90. Ibid., II.iii.2.

91. Origen, *Contra Celsum* V.xv.

92. Origen, *Prin.* I.i.5.

93. Ibid., II.x.8.

94. Neither is the body's future participation in the reward of the soul emphasized by Origen; Origen argues against a physical interpretation of the millennium—the traditional point at which to image delights of the senses—and for a purely spiritual understanding of the "promises" (*Prin.* II.xi.2-3).

95. Origen, *In Matt. Comm.* Series 72, in Tollinton, *Selections,* p. 200.

96. Origen, *Prin.* III.vi.9.

97. Ibid., I.v.7.

98. Ibid., I.v.5.

99. Origen, *In Matt. Comm.* 15.1, 348ff.

100. See the excellent discussion of the evidence for Origen's self-mutilation and his later treatment of Matt. 19:12 in Gerard Caspary, *Politics and Exegesis: Origen and the Two Swords* (University of California Press, 1979), pp. 59-63.

101. Ibid., pp. 59-60.

102. Eusebius, *Historia Ecclesiastica* VI.8.1.

103. Origen, *On Prayer*, in H. Chadwick, *Alexandrian Christianity*, p. 257. Cf. Clement's instructions for prayer in which the body is engaged in the effort (*Strom.* VII.vii.40).

104. Origen, *Dialogue*, in H. Chadwick, *Alexandrian Christianity*, p. 445.

105. Ibid., p. 453.

106. Ibid., p. 452.

107. Origen, *Prin.* I.i.8.

108. Origen, *Super Isaiam*, in Tollinton, *Selections*, p. 234.

109. Origen, *Dialogue*, p. 454.

110. Origen, *Exhortation*, p. 422.

111. Origen, *Dialogue*, p. 453.

112. Ibid., p. 410.

III. HUMAN NATURE AND EMBODIMENT IN AUGUSTINE

1. Augustine, *Confessions* X.8; translations from *Confessions* are from Rex Warner (tr.), *The Confessions of St. Augustine* (New American Library, 1963).

2. Ibid., VI.6.

3. Augustine, *De correptione et gratia* 24.

4. Augustine, *Conf.* I.19; for a contemporary description of infantile anxiety, see the remark of the behavioral psychologist Jean Piaget, *The Construction of Reality in the Child* (Ballantine Books, 1954), p. 329: "It is striking to observe . . . how the nursling, when his mother is getting him ready for his meals, counts very little on her for obtaining the object of his desires; he makes a great fuss, becomes impatient, tries to grasp the bottle . . . but is not at all content to await the normal course of events. It all happens as though he depended only on himself to attain his goal."

5. Ibid., I.9.

6. Augustine, *Epistula* CXL.xxiii.56: "The rational creature, whether in the form of an angelic spirit or of a human soul, has been so made that it cannot itself be the good by which it is made happy; but it is made happy if its mutability is changed into an immutable good, and if it turn away from this it is miserable. This turning away is its vice; its virtue is the turning toward this good. Our nature, therefore, is not evil of itself, since the creature is rational by the life of the spirit, even when deprived of that good the participation of which makes it happy, that is to say even when vicious it is better than that body which holds the chief place among bodies, namely than this light which is perceived by the eyes

of the flesh, since it too is itself a body. But incorporeal nature is superior to
every body whatever it may be, and this not by its mass; for mass is a property of
bodies alone, but by a certain force by which it rises to heights inaccessible to
any and every notion drawn by the mind from the senses of the body." See also
In Ps. CXXI.1: "Every love has a force of its own. Love cannot be inactive in a
lover, it cannot but lead him in some direction. If you would know the character
of a person's love, see where it is leading."

7. Augustine, *Conf.* I.1.

8. Augustine, *Enchiridion* 31.117.

9. Augustine, *Conf.* VI.6; see also *Ep.* CXL.ii.3ff: "There is a kind of life of
humankind, wholly of the senses and given up to the joys of the flesh, which
shuns anything which is an offense to the flesh and pursues nothing but pleasure.
The happiness to be found in such a life is temporary. *It is a necessity to begin
with this sort of life;* to persist in it however is an act of the will. It is into this life
that a child is thrown at his birth."

10. See Norman P. Williams, *Ideas of the Fall and of Original Sin* (London:
Longmans, Green & Co., 1927).

11. Augustine, *De civitate Dei* XIX.4.

12. Augustine, *De musica* VI.11.29.

13. Augustine, *Conf.* VII.xii.

14. Augustine, *De civ. Dei* XIX.13.

15. Augustine, *Conf.* VIII.8-11.

16. Ibid., VIII.11.

17. See also Augustine, *Conf.* VIII.6: "The law of sin is the strong force of
habit."

18. Ibid.

19. Augustine, *De doctrina christiana* I.8: "Et quoniam omnes qui de Deo
cogitant, vivum aliquid cogitant, illi soli possunt non absurda et indigna
existimare de Deo, qui vitam ipsam cogitant."

20. Augustine, *Conf.* X.4: "Quid sum cum mihi bene est, nisi sugens lac, tum
aut fruens te cibo?" See also Augustine's description of his conversion as
"relaxing a little from myself": "cessavi de me paululum" (*Conf.* VII.14).

21. Augustine, *De trinitate* XV.xxi.41.

22. Augustine, *De doct. christ.* III.x.15, 16.

23. Augustine, *Soliloquies* I.1.2.

24. Augustine told us enough about his attachments to other human beings in
his early life to indicate the extent to which friendship inevitably and
automatically became, not simply relationship, but both concupiscence, or the
grasping longing to possess the other (*Conf.* II.2), and inability to differentiate
his life from the life of the person he loved (his friend: *Conf.* IV.4, 6; his mother:
Conf. IX.12). This early tendency to swallow and be swallowed by friends is the
motivation for Augustine's mature description of friendship as "loving the
neighbor in God" (discussed above, p. 66). A precise novelistic description of

this condition is given in Jean Dutourd's *The Horrors of Love* (Doubleday & Co., 1967).

25. Augustine, *De trin.* XIV.xiv.18.

26. See A.-M. Bonnardiere, "La date du 'De concupiscentia' de s. Augustin," *Revue des Études Augustiniennes* I (1959): 122.

27. Augustine, *De libero arbitrio* II.xvi.41.

28. Augustine, *Ep.* CXL.xxiii.56.

29. Augustine, *De quantitate animae* xxxiii.70f.: "First then, as anyone can easily see, the soul quickens by its presence this earthly and mortal body, it gathers it into one and holds it in one, it does not allow it to fall apart and decay; it causes food to be distributed equably among the members of the body, allotting to each what is proper to it; it preserves its harmony and measure, not only in beauty of form, but also in growth and reproduction."

30. Augustine, *Ep.* CXVIII.13.

31. Augustine, *Ep.* CXXXVII.3.11.

32. Augustine, *Solil.* I.xiv.24.

33. Augustine, *Retractions* I.16.

34. Augustine, *Ep.* CXXXVII.3.

35. Augustine, *In Joannis Evangelium* XXIII.10.

36. Augustine, *De mendacio* vii.10.

37. Augustine, *De moribus Ecclesiae catholicae et de moribus Manichaeorum* I.xi.18: "We seek to attain God by loving him; we attain to him, not by becoming entirely what he is, but in nearness to him, and in wonderful and *sensible contact with him,* and in being inwardly illuminated and occupied by his truth and holiness."

38. Augustine, *Conf.* X.6.

39. Augustine, *De trin.* XII.5.5.

40. Augustine, *De mor. eccl.* I.xxi.39.

41. Augustine, *De civ. Dei* XIV.15.

42. Ibid., XIX.22.

43. Ibid.,

44. Augustine, *Ep.* CCXLIII.11.

45. Augustine, *De civ. Dei* XIII.6: "asperum sensum et contra naturam."

46. In contrast to Augustine's frankly imaginative picture of sex in the Garden of Eden (*De civ. Dei* XIV.26), human sexuality in its fallen condition displays all the embarrassment and pain of the divided will: "Sometimes the impulse is an unwanted intruder, sometimes it abandons the eager lover, and desire cools off in the body while it is still at boiling heat in the mind. Thus strangely concupiscence refuses to be a servant . . . even to the concupiscence for lascivious indulgence; and although on the whole it is totally opposed to the mind's control, it is quite often divided against itself. It arouses the mind, but does not follow its own lead by arousing the body" (ibid., XIV. 16).

47. Augustine, *De trin.* XII.9.14; see note 51 below.

48. Augustine, *De civ. Dei* XIII.3.

49. Ibid., XIII.10.

50. Augustine, *De trin.* XII.9.14.

51. Ibid.: "The soul conducts everything through its own body, which it only partly possesses, when it struggles to assert something of its own over against the laws with which the universe is administered. So, having delighted in corporeal forms and movements, which it cannot have within itself, the soul is wrapped in their images, which it has fixed in memory, and is perverted and disgraced. . . . When, in fact, the soul does anything for the sake of obtaining things sensed through the body on account of its lust for experiencing or excelling or handling, *so that it places in them the end of its own good,* it does to its disgrace whatever it does. It commits a sin of fornication against its own body."

52. Augustine, *Conf.* X.6.

53. Ibid., VI.6-16.

54. Augustine, *In Ps.* 41.

55. Augustine, *De civ. Dei* XIII.16.

56. Augustine, *De utilitate jejunii* iv.

57. Augustine, *De doct. christ.* I.24.24.

58. Augustine, *In Joann. Evang.* XXVII.5.

59. Augustine, *Contra Faust. Mani.* XI.3.

60. Augustine, *Ep.* XCII.

61. Augustine, *De civ. Dei* XXII.29.

62. Ibid.

63. See above, p. 73.

64. None of the senses perfectly models the resurrection experience of nonhabituating delight; even vision, although its presentational simultaneity is accurate, "is nowhere wholly present . . . [but] is extended through a series of spatial points" (Augustine, *De libero arbitrio* ii.14.38).

65. Augustine, *Sermons* CCXL.3.

66. Augustine, *De doct. christ.* I.25.26–I.26.27.

67. Ibid., I.24.24.

68. Augustine, *De civ. Dei* XV.7.2.

69. Augustine, *De genesi ad litteram* XII.35.68.

70. See my earlier work, *Augustine on the Body* (Missoula, Montana: Scholars Press, 1979), for a fuller discussion of Augustine's view of the body and sexuality.

71. Augustine, *Contra Julianum* III.7.15.

72. Augustine, *De continentia* IX.22.

73. Augustine, *Conf.* II.2.

74. Augustine, *De bono conjugali* xxiii.29.

75. Ibid., vii.8.

76. Augustine, *Serm.* CCXLIII.8.

IV. EAST AND WEST AFTER AUGUSTINE

1. Augustine, *Epistula* CXXIII.3.14.
2. Augustine, *De vera religione* XXV.47; see also *De utilitate credendi* 16.34.
3. Augustine, *De civitate Dei* XXII.8.
4. As Clement calls it: see *Strom.* VII.ii.11.
5. Plotinus describes the realm of intellect as "boiling with life" (*Enneads* VI.5.12).
6. William C. Bark, *Origins of the Medieval World* (Stanford University Press, 1958), pp. 89ff.
7. Ibid., p. 70.
8. Ibid., pp. 5ff.
9. See Irenaeus, *Adv. haer.* IV.xviii.5.
10. Cyril of Alexandria, *Epistula* 17.
11. Cyril of Alexandria, *De incarnatione unigeniti.*
12. Ernest Brehaut, in the Introduction to his translation of Gregory of Tours, *History of the Franks* (W. W. Norton & Co., 1969), p. xxi et passim.
13. Boethius, *The Consolation of Philosophy*, Bk. I, prose 4; tr. by Richard Green (Bobbs-Merrill Co., 1963).
14. Gregory of Tours, *History of the Franks* II.40.
15. Ibid., VIII.34; see also VI.6, VI.29.
16. Ibid., IV.31.
17. Ibid., VI.8.
18. Selections from the *Book of Miracles*, in Gregory of Tours, *History of the Franks*, p. 252.
19. Ibid., p. 259.
20. Gregory the Great, *Dialogues* II.23.
21. Ibid., II.35.
22. Ibid., II.38.
23. Julian, Roman emperor (d. A.D. 363), *Against the Galileans.*
24. Gregory the Great, *Dialogues* II.xxiii.
25. Bede, *A History of the English Church and People*, tr. and with an Introduction by Leo Sherley-Price (Penguin Books, 1955), I.26. Quotations from this book are copyright © 1955 by Leo Sherley-Price and are reprinted by permission of Penguin Books, Ltd.
26. Ibid., III.9.
27. Ibid., II.1.
28. Ibid., IV.19.
29. Ibid., II.13.
30. Quoted in Leo Sherley-Price (tr.), *Bede: A History of the English Church and People*, p. 19.
31. See, for example, Gregory the Great, *Dialogues* IV.3: "For that our soul lives after the death of the body, reason teaches us, assisted and helped by faith: for God created three kinds of spirits having life. One is altogether spiritual

without body; another with a body, but yet which does not die with the body; the third that which is both joined to the body and also dies with the body. The spirits that have no bodies are the angels; they that have bodies but do not die with them are the souls of human beings; those that have bodies and die with them are the souls of cattle and beasts. Human beings, therefore, as they are created in the middle state, inferior to angels and superior to beasts, partake of both; having immortality of soul with the angels and mortality of body with the beasts, until the day of doom; for then the glory of the resurrection will take away and consume the mortality of the body; for being then reunited to the soul it will be preserved forever; as the soul joined to the body is preserved for God."

32. Vladimir Lossky, *The Mystical Theology of the Eastern Church* (1957; St. Vladimir's Seminary Press, 1976), p. 9.

33. Quoted by M. J. Le Guillou, *The Spirit of Eastern Orthodoxy* (Hawthorn Books, 1962), p. 99.

34. Jaroslav Pelikan, *The Spirit of Eastern Christendom 600-1700;* The Christian Tradition, Vol. II (University of Chicago Press, 1974), p. 32.

35. Gregory of Nyssa, *Commentary on the Canticles;* tr. by Le Guillou, *Spirit of Eastern Orthodoxy*, p. 31.

36. John of Damascus, *The Orthodox Faith* I.2.

37. Maximus the Confessor, *Scholia on the Divine Names of Dionysius the Areopagite* 3.1.

38. Simeon the New Theologian, *Orations* 26; Pelikan, *Spirit of Eastern Christendom*, p. 258.

39. Maximus the Confessor, *Theological and Polemical Opuscula* 22.

40. Maximus the Confessor, *Questions to Thalassius on the Scripture* 6. II Cor. 3:18 was often quoted to support deification language: "But we all beholding (*katoptrizomenoi*, mirroring) the glory of the Lord with open face are transformed into the same image from glory to glory as by the spirit of the Lord."

41. The idea of an evenly graded ascent through the levels of being will return to the West, but I do not know of a single Western treatise between Augustine's description of a discursive ascent in *De quantitate animae* and that of Bonaventure in *Itinerarium mentis in Deum*, which gives such a description.

42. Lossky, *Mystical Theology*, p. 243.

43. Ibid.

44. Gregory of Nyssa, *De opificio hominis* XII.9, 10; *A Select Library of the Nicene and Post-Nicene Fathers*, Vol. V (Christian Literature Co., 1893).

45. St. John Climacus, *The Ladder of Divine Ascent;* tr. by Lazarus Moore (Harper & Brothers, 1959), p. 264. For a variety of locations by patristic authors of the part of human being which corresponds to the image of God, see Lossky, *Mystical Theology*, pp. 115f.

46. Gregory of Nyssa, *De op. hom.* XVI.17. See also John of Damascus, *The Orthodox Faith* IV.16: "On what grounds, then, do we show reverence to each other, except that we have been made according to God's image?"

47. Ibid., XVII.4.

48. Ibid., XVII.4, 5.

49. Gregory of Nyssa, *De virginitate* VIII.

50. Ibid., IX.

51. Ibid., XIII.

52. Ibid., XXI.

53. Cf. Plato's observation, often forgotten in Western asceticism, that "each pleasure or pain nails [the soul] as with a nail to the body and rivets it on and makes it corporeal " (*Phaedo* 83).

54. Gregory of Nyssa, *De virginitate* XXVI.

55. Ibid., XXVII.

56. Ibid., XXVIII.1.

57. Ibid., XXIX.1.

58. Ibid., XXX.29.

59. Ibid., XXX.30; cf. XVII.4, quoted above, p. 102.

60. Charles Journet, "Saint Augustin et l'exégèse traditionelle du 'corpus spirituale,' " *Augustinus Magister* 2 (1954), p. 886.

61. See also Gregory of Nyssa, *In Christi resurrectionem, Oratio* III.

62. Gregory Palamas, *Homilies*; Lossky, *Mystical Theology*, pp. 224f.

63. Lossky, *Mystical Theology*, p. 209.

64. See, for example, Pelikan's statement that the controversy over icons became "a new version of the christological debates"; *Spirit of Eastern Christendom*, p. 91.

65. Nicephorus, in the *Antirrheticus* 1.28, defines an image as "a likeness of an archetype, having impressed upon it the form of what it represents by similarity, differing from it only by the difference of essence in accordance with the materials [of which they are made]; or an imitation and similitude of the archetype, differing in essence and substance; or a product of some technical skill, shaped in accordance with the imitation of the archetype, but differing from it in essence and substance."

66. L. W. Barnard, *The Graeco-Roman and Oriental Background of the Iconoclastic Controversy* (Leiden: E. J. Brill, 1974), p. 102.

67. Ibid.

68. John of Damascus, *Orations on the Images*; Barnard, *Iconoclastic Controversy*, p. 103.

69. Constantine Cavarnos, *Orthodox Iconography* (Institute for Byzantine and Modern Greek Studies, 1977), p. 53, n. 18.

70. John Cassian, *Conferences* X.3; in O. Chadwick, *Western Asceticism*, pp. 234f.

71. See Athansius, *De incarnatione* 14.

72. John of Damascus, *The Orthodox Faith* IV.16; tr in Cavarnos, *Orthodox Iconography*, p. 51.

73. Ibid.

74. See the quotation from Simeon the New Theologian, above, p. 96.

75. Nicephorus, *Greater Apology for the Holy Images* 70.

76. Gregory of Nyssa, *On Theodore the Martyr;* in Pelikan, *Spirit of Eastern Christendom,* p. 104.

77. Quoted in Barnard, *Iconoclastic Controversy,* p. 101.

78. Rudolph Arnheim, *Visual Thinking* (University of California Press, 1969).

79. Cavarnos, *Orthodox Iconography,* pp. 36ff.

80. Ibid., p. 53.

81. Cf. Plotinus, *Enneads* IV.3.8: "We are what we desire and what we look at."

82. An interesting parallel to the conflict of the Eastern Church is the mini-iconoclastic controversy of Claudius of Turin and Theodimir. Claudius' iconoclasm uses an argument comparable to that of Eastern iconoclasts—a call to transcend material objects of devotion in order to worship a transcendent God. Claudius used all his powers of invective to express his scorn of "crutches." Quoting Paul's "even though we once regarded Christ according to the flesh, we now regard him thus no longer," Claudius argued against people he called the "adherents of superstition and false religion":

> Against them we must reply that if they wish to adore all wood fashioned in the shape of a cross because Christ hung on a cross, then it is fitting for them to adore many other things which Christ did in the flesh. He hung on the cross scarcely six hours, but he was in the Virgin's womb nine lunar months and more than eleven days, a total of two hundred and seventy-six solar days, that is, nine months and more than six days. Let virgin girls therefore be adored, because a Virgin gave birth to Christ. Let mangers be adored, because as soon as he was born he was laid in a manger. Let old rags be adored, because immediately after he was born he was wrapped in old rags. Let boats be adored, because he often sailed in boats, taught the throngs from a small boat, slept in a boat, from a boat commanded the winds, and to the right of a fishing boat ordered them to cast the net when that great prophetic draught of fish was made. Let asses be adored, because he came to Jerusalem sitting on an ass. Let lambs be adored, because it was written of him, "Behold the lamb of God who takes away the sins of the world." But those infamous devotees of perverse doctrines prefer to eat the living lambs and adore only the ones painted on the wall.

(The quotation is from Claudius of Turin, *Reply and Defense to Theodomir;* in George E. McCracken and Allen Cabaniss [eds.], *Early Medieval Theology,* The Library of Christian Classics, Vol. IX; Westminster Press, 1957, p. 244.)

83. Quoted in Barnard, *Iconoclastic Controversy,* pp. 7-8.

V. A THIRTEENTH-CENTURY SYNTHESIS

1. M.-D. Chenu, *Nature, Man, and Society in the Twelfth Century* (University of Chicago Press, 1968), p. 15.

2. Peter Brown, "Society and the Supernatural: A Medieval Change," *Daedalus*, Spring 1975, pp. 133-151.

3. *The Little Flowers of St. Francis*, tr. by Raphael Brown (Doubleday & Co., Image Books, 1958), p. 90.

4. *The Considerations on the Holy Stigmata*, in Brown (tr.), *Little Flowers*, p. 194.

5. Bonaventure, *The Mind's Road to God*, tr. by George Boas (Bobbs-Merrill Co., 1953), pp. 4-5. Quotations from this book are copyright © 1953 by The Bobbs-Merrill Company, Inc., and are reprinted by permission.

6. Ibid., p. 10.

7. Ibid., p. 13.

8. By which, for example, we can contemplate God not only *through* sensible objects, but *in* them, because he is in them in "essence, potency, and presence" (ibid., p. 14).

9. Bonaventure, *The Mind's Road to God* (Boas tr.), p. 18.

10. Ibid., p. 26.

11. Ibid., p. 29.

12. Ibid., p. 35.

13. Ibid., p. 40.

14. Ibid., p. 41.

15. Ibid., p. 44.

16. Etienne Gilson, *The Philosophy of St. Bonaventure* (Sheed & Ward, 1938).

17. Thomas Aquinas, *Summa Theologiae* Ia. 2, 2, ad 1; hereafter referred to as *Summa*. Translations from the *Summa*, unless otherwise stated, are from the Blackfriars edition (McGraw-Hill Book Co., 1964ff.), 60 vols.

18. Ibid., Ia. 1.

19. Timothy Suttor, Introduction to the *Summa*, Blackfriars ed., Vol. XI, p. xvii.

20. As observed by Paul Durbin in his Introduction to the *Summa*, Vol. XII, Thomas' purpose in the Treatise on Human Intelligence (Ia. 84-89) is to "defend genuinely natural knowledge from absorption into some supposed higher mode of knowing" (p. xxi).

21. Aquinas, II *Contra Gentiles*, 4; Thomas Gilby (tr.), *St. Thomas Aquinas, Theological Texts* (Oxford University Press, 1955), p. 6.

22. Aquinas, Exposition, *de Trinitate* ii. 3.

23. Aquinas, *Summa* Ia. 2ae. 101, 1.

24. Aquinas, I *Contra Gentiles*, 8; see also Thomas' statement that, in fact, analogies are less apt to deceive if they are clearly "gross understatements," rather than if they are "noble figures" which might be seen as characterizing God. *Summa* Ia. 1, 9, ad 3.

25. Aquinas, *Summa* Ia. 84, 8; see also *Disputations*, xvi, *de Malo*, ad 3: "Imagining goes with thinking so long as we are in this present life, however spiritual the knowledge. Even God is known through the images of his effects." See also *Opusc.* xvi, *de Trinitate*, vi. 2, ad 5: "The image is the principle of our knowledge. It is that from which our intellectual activity begins, *not as a passing stimulus, but as an enduring foundation.* When the imagination is choked, so also is our theological knowledge."

26. Aquinas, III *Contra Gentiles*, 149.

27. Thomas Gilby (tr.), *St. Thomas Aquinas: Philosophical Texts* (Oxford University Press, 1960), p. 193. First published 1951. Quotations from this book are reprinted by permission of Oxford University Press.

28. Aquinas, *Summa* Ia. 75, 4.

29. Ibid., Ia. 76, 3.

30. Ibid., Ia. 76, 1.

31. Ibid., Ia. 75, 3.

32. Ibid., Ia. 75, 7.

33. Aquinas, Commentary, II *ad Corinthos* xii, lect. 1.

34. Aquinas, Commentary, II *de Anima*, lect. 19. See also *Summa* Ia. 76, 5: "Among human beings, those have the finer minds who have the more delicate sense of touch. A rare mind goes with bodily refinement."

35. Aquinas, *Summa* Ia. 76, 1.

36. Ibid., Ia. 84, 7.

37. Ibid., Ia. 84, 4.

38. Aquinas, *Opusc.* xiii, *Compendium Theologiae*, 104.

39. Aquinas, *Summa* Ia. 76, 1.

40. James Collins, *The Thomistic Philosophy of the Angels* (Catholic University of America Press, 1947), p. 14.

41. Aquinas, *Summa* Ia. 22, 4.

42. Aquinas, III *Contra Gentiles*, 149; see also *Summa* Ia. 23, 8.

43. Etienne Gilson, *The Christian Philosophy of St. Augustine* (Random House, 1960), p. 121.

44. Aquinas, *Disputations*, vi, *de Potentia*, 1.

45. Ibid.

46. Aquinas, *Summa* IIIa. 43, 2.

47. St. Thomas might have said with Rainer Maria Rilke, "We had a different conception of the marvelous; we found that if everything happened naturally that would always be the most marvelous " (*The Notebooks of Malte Laurids Brigge;* W. W. Norton & Co., 1949, p. ii). See also Aquinas, Exposition, *Apostles Creed:* "If you say, but no one has seen miracles performed, then I answer, that once upon a time everybody worshipped false gods and persecuted Christians, and then afterwards were converted including the wise, noble, powerful, by a few unlettered preachers. Either this was miraculous or not. If so,

then the point is granted; if not, then I ask, what greater miracle could there have been than to convert so many without miracles?"

48. Aquinas, III *Contra Gentiles*, 149; see also *Summa* Ia.-2ae. 113, 3: "God moves a person to justice in a manner which accords with the condition of his human nature."

49. Aquinas, Exposition, *de Trinitate* ii. 3.

50. Aquinas, *Summa* Ia.-2ae. 110, 2.

51. Ibid., Ia. lxxxiv, 3. See the definition of "natural" (Blackfriars edition of the *Summa*, Vol. XI, Glossary, p. 272): "The essential constitution of a thing. As contrasted with the opposed or violent, the principle of spontaneous motion from within, whether conscious or unconscious, nondeliberate or deliberate."

52. Aquinas, *Opusc.* xiii, *Compendium Theologiae*, 151.

53. Aquinas, *Summa* 2a.-2ae. 28, 3.

54. Ibid., Ia. 1, 1.

55. Ibid., 2a.-2ae. 141, 4.

56. Ibid., Ia. 90, 4.

57. Aquinas, IV *Contra Gentiles*, 52.

58. Aquinas, *Summa* IIIa. 14, 3, ad 2; see also *Compendium Theologiae*, 196.

59. Aquinas, *Summa* Ia. 90, 4, ad 3.

60. Aquinas, IV *Contra Gentiles*, 79; see also *Opusc.* xiii, *Compendium Theologiae*, 151, quoted, p. 128.

61. This is a highly significant conclusion, and one in which Thomas departs from Augustine's interpretation of *concupiscentia* as transmitted by the physical act of sexual intercourse. Thomas cannot accept that a spiritual flaw is transmitted through a physical act. See *Disputations* IV, *de Malo* 6, ad 16.

62. Aquinas, *Summa* Ia. 98, 2.

63. Ibid., Ia. 98, 1.

64. Ibid.

65. Ibid.

66. Ibid.

67. Ibid., Ia. 92, 3.

68. Ibid., Ia. 92, 1.

69. Ibid., Ia. 92, 2.

70. Ibid., Ia. 93, 5.

71. Ibid., Ia.-2ae. 4, 6.

72. Ibid., Ia.-2ae. 4, 3.

73. The difficulty at the heart of Thomas' hierarchical interpretation of the sexes is apparent here: on this account, men ought to possess more potential for happiness than women since they possess stronger rational powers and so, presumably, can achieve the rational end more readily and to a greater degree.

74. Aquinas, *Quodlibets*, viii, 1.

75. Aquinas, *Compendium Theologiae*, 168; Gilby, *Theological Texts*, p. 409.

76. Aquinas, *Summa* Ia.-2ae. 3, 3.

VI. FOUR TYPES OF CHRISTIAN ASCETICISM

1. Augustine, *De civitate Dei* XV.7.

2. Ambrose, *De virginitate* I.2. See also Augustine, *De continentia* i: "Continence is a gift of God. . . . Unless God give it, it is impossible for anyone to be continent."

3. Palladius, *The Paradise of the Holy Fathers, The Lausiac History of Palladius*, Vol. VI, J. Armitage Robinson, ed. (London: Chatto & Windus, 1907), p. 78.

4. *The Sayings of the Fathers*, in O. Chadwick, *Western Asceticism*, p. 43.

5. Evagrius Ponticus, *The Praktikos*, tr. by John E. Bamberger (Kalamazoo, Mich.: Cistercian Publications, 1970), p. 61.

6. Ibid., p. 92.

7. Ibid., p. 43.

8. Ibid., p. 50.

9. Ibid., p. 78.

10. Ibid., p. 53.

11. Ibid., p. 51: "The state of prayer can aptly be described as a habitual state of imperturable calm *(apatheia)*."

12. Cassian, *Conferences* 1.7, in O. Chadwick, *Western Asceticism:* "Fasting, watching, meditation of Scripture, nakedness, poverty are . . . not the end of our discipline but the means to that end."

13. Evagrius Ponticus, *Praktikos* 16: "When the soul desires to seek after a variety of foods, *then it is time* to afflict it with bread and water that it may learn to be grateful for a mere morsel of bread."

14. Ibid., 53.

15. Palladius, *Lausiac History* (Robinson ed.), pp. 239-240. See also *Praktikos* 29: "The human body is like a coat. If you treat it carefully it will last a long time. If you neglect it, it will fall into tatters."

16. Evagrius Ponticus, *Praktikos* 89.

17. Ibid., 11. See also Palladius, *Lausiac History* (Robinson ed.), p. 87, for acknowledgment that "spiritual excellence" is directly evident in health of body: "There are many things which testify concerning spiritual excellence, such as the color of the face which blossoms with ascetic labors, and the manner in which the apparel is put on, and a peaceable manner, and a mode of speech which is not inflated, and modesty of countenance, and a discourse which is not crooked, and cheerfulness of the mind, and an understanding which is full of knowledge."

18. Cassian, *Conferences* I.7.

19. Ibid., I.21.

20. Ibid., I.20.

21. Palladius, *Lausiac History* (Robinson ed.), p. 82.

22. Pachomius, *Vita(e) Pachomii* I.120; F. Halkin (ed.), *Sancti Pachomii Vitae* (Subsidia Hagiographica, XIX, 1932).

23. The solitaries of the Egyptian desert were not unaware of the danger of preoccupation with one's own psyche; the characteristic distortions and temptations of the struggle for self-knowledge and self-mastery are treated again and again in the *apophthegmata*. These temptations are analyzed as envy and "indiscretion." Envy is the temptation to forget one's own "rung" and attempt to occupy the "rung" of another; indiscretion is putting all one's attention on the "tools" of one's profession so that excesses destroy virtues: "too rigorous solitude, too rigorous abstinence, too much faith in visions" (Cassian, *Conferences* I.23).

24. Ibid., I.13.

25. Benedict, *Rule*, Prologue.

26. Cassian, *Conferences* 10; see also 7.

27. Basil, *Rule (Regulae brevius tractatae)* 13.

28. Benedict, *Rule* 5.

29. Ibid., 68.

30. Ibid., 64.

31. Ibid.

32. Ibid., 33.

33. Augustine, *De continentia* ix.22.

34. Ibid., xxii.26.

35. Augustine, *De utilitate jejunii* iv.

36. Augustine, *De libero arbitrio* II.25.39.

37. Augustine, *De util. jejun.* i.

38. Ibid., ii.

39. Augustine, *De quantitate animae* xxv.79.

40. Ibid., xxiii.70.

41. Augustine, *Epistula* CXVIII.iii.

42. *The Spiritual Exercises of St. Ignatius*, tr. by Anthony Mottola (Doubleday & Co., Image Books, 1964), p. 47.

43. Ibid., p. 41.

44. Ibid.

45. Ibid., p. 40.

46. Ibid., p. 71.

47. Ibid., p. 62.

48. Ibid., p. 39.

49. Ibid., p. 94.

50. Ibid., p. 57.

51. Ibid., p. 59.

52. Ibid., p. 102.

53. Ibid., p. 103.

VII. TOWARD A NEW ASCETICISM

1. *The Sayings of the Fathers*, in O. Chadwick, *Western Asceticism*, p. 109.

2. *Heraclidis Paradeisos* I.

3. Augustine, *De utilitate jejunii* i.

4. Ibid., iii; see also Ignatius Loyola, *Spiritual Exercises*, p. 61.

5. See, for example, Jerry Mander, *Four Arguments for the Elimination of Television* (William Morrow & Co., Quill Paperbacks, 1978), and Wilson Bryan Key, *Subliminal Seduction* (New American Library, 1974).

6. *The Sayings of the Fathers*, in O. Chadwick, *Western Asceticism*, pp. 74-75: "Stop all this discipline, take a little food at the proper times, recover your strength, join in the worship of God for a little, and turn your mind to the Lord—for this is a thing you cannot conquer by your own efforts. The human body is like a coat. If you treat it carefully, it will last a long time. If you neglect it, it will fall into tatters."

7. This statement about Antony's healthy and youthful appearance at the end of twenty years of austerities must be balanced with his apparent attitude of "shame" about his embodiment, which caused him, Athanasius says, "to blush every time he had to eat or satisfy any other bodily function" (*Vita Antonii*, 45). It is clear that the good of the body was not Antony's goal, but yet his consciously chosen asceticism resulted in his body's health and well-being.

8. For treatments of permanent celibacy as "existential disablement from marriage," see Roger Balducelli, O.S.F.S., The Decision for Celibacy," *Theological Studies*, Vol. 36, No. 2 (June 1975), pp. 219-242, and Edward Schillebeeckx, *Celibacy*, tr. by C. A. L. Jarrot (Sheed & Ward, 1968).

9. Clement, *Stromateis* VII.xii.72; in H. Chadwick, *Alexandrian Christianity*, p. 138.

10. Calvin, *Institutes of the Christian Religion* II.viii.43.

11. Cassian, *Conferences* I.4.

12. Ibid., I.7.

13. H. R. Niebuhr, *The Meaning of Revelation* (Macmillan Co., 1941), p. 81.

14. Augustine, *De doctrina christiana* I.8: "Only they can think of God without absurdity who think of God as life itself."

INDEX